THE BOY'S BOOK OF
POSITIVE
QUOTATIONS

by Steve Deger
Illustrated by Queenie Chan

Fairview Press
Minneapolis

Published by Fairview Press, 2450 Riverside Avenue, Minneapolis, Minnesota 55454. For a free catalog of Fairview Press titles, call toll-free 1-800-544-8207, or visit our website at www.fairviewpress.org.

Fairview Press is a division of Fairview Health Services, a community-focused health system, affiliated with the University of Minnesota, providing a complete range of services, from the prevention of illness and injury to care for the most complex medical conditions.

Library of Congress Cataloging-in-Publication Data

Deger, Steve, 1966-
  The boy's book of positive quotations / by Steve Deger ;
illustrated by Queenie Chan.
      p. cm.
  ISBN 978-1-57749-189-7 (hardcover : alk. paper)
  1. Conduct of life—Quotations, maxims, etc. 2. Boys—Conduct of life.
  I. Chan, Queenie. II. Title.
  PN6084.C556D43 2009
  646.7—dc22

                                    2009019093

Interior design: Ryan Scheife, Mayfly Design (www.mayflydesign.net)
Illustrations: Queenie Chan (www.queeniechan.com)
Pico Mundo Grille logo © Dean Koontz. Used with permission.

Printed in Canada
First Printing: July 2009

13   12   11   10   09   7   6   5   4   3   2

CONTENTS

INTRODUCTION

ATTICUS SMYTHE AND HIS SECRET SENSEI

Have you ever wished you could have your own personal sidekick? A training partner to help you get a starting position on a sports team? Somebody who could step in and keep the jerks at school from hassling you? A "wingman" who could help you look cool in the eyes of that one cutie in your class?

In this book, that's what our hero Atticus gets when a mysterious ninja starts texting him. Her messages come in the form of little proverbs—each one containing a coded secret to living an honorable life. And when she's not texting him from the sidelines, she's coaching him on martial arts, helping him find the ultimate Halloween costume, cheering him on in sports, and letting

him lean on her at times when everything in life pretty much *blows*.

Chances are, your life isn't like Atticus'. You don't have some hottie ninja following you around, ready to whip out her sword and shred whatever's bugging you on any given day. But that doesn't mean you have to go it alone. Every dude out there—from the top competitors in the X Games to the stars of the X-Men movies—has to deal with the same things that confront you. Doubt. Stress. Frustration. The urge to quit. And yet all of these men have overcome these challenges to ultimately find their inner heroes.

So, rather than giving you *one* personal sidekick, we're giving you about 500 of them. We've compiled the advice and insights of famous men from the arts, business, journalism, movies, music, science and exploration, sports, and more. Each of them presents his life lessons within the pages of this book—all for you to read when and if you need them.

How (or if) you use this book is up to you. Maybe you're more interested in finding out what happens to Atticus than you are in learning how to bring your own dreams to life. That's cool. Or maybe you're curious to see how your place of worship might help you form your own rock band (in which case, we highly recommend skipping straight to Chapter 22).

Whether you find inspiration from this book doesn't really matter. What matters is that you find it somewhere, every day, for the rest of your life. Find it from a supportive family member, a teacher, a coach, or a member of your faith community. Or search for inspiration deep inside, from that little inner voice inside you that keeps telling you that you're destined for something big. *Really* big.

In the end, it's that little inner voice inside you that matters most. It knows more about you, and what you're capable of, than anyone else in the world.

THE 1ST NINJA SECRET TO BEING A TOTALLY UNSTOPPABLE KID

HOW TO BE FIRST AT ANYTHING

(BEING BRAVE AND DARING)

Everybody wants to be number one, but there's rarely a long line to be first. Sure, it's cool to be the top scorer at Guitar Hero or the homerun king in a baseball game. But the difference between being number one and being first is a backpack full of guts.

It takes courage to be the first person to do something. Going first means all eyes are watching you. So there's double pressure: you don't want to blow it and you don't want to let people down. Getting first in line, though, can boost your confidence and win you a ton of admirers.

Here are just a few things you could do first:

- Be the first student to stand up in front of the class and give your speech. Everyone will think you're totally brave. (And you'll get it out of the way!)

- Be the first to invite the new kid to sit with you at lunch. That new guy might end up being the funniest kid in your class, and you'll look cooler just because people know you are friends.

- Be the first to spin across the floor at your school dance. Your friends won't be far behind.

- Be the first to sign up for a new activity at school. Maybe staffing the school yearbook sounds boring, but you might develop a lifelong love of photography.

What you do says a lot about who you are. If you want people to think you're gutsy, interesting, and cool, show them by being first. ●

I guess we all like to be recognized not for one piece of fireworks, but for the ledger of our daily work.

—**NEIL ARMSTRONG**, ASTRONAUT AND FIRST PERSON ON THE MOON

Coming together is a beginning. Keeping together is progress. Working together is success.

—**HENRY FORD**, FIRST BUSINESSMAN TO DEVELOP AN ASSEMBLY LINE

I like to be against the odds. I'm not afraid to be lonely at the top. With me, it's just the satisfaction of the game.

—**BARRY BONDS**, FIRST FOUR-TIME MVP IN MAJOR LEAGUE BASEBALL

Our American professors like their literature clear and cold and pure and very dead.

—**SINCLAIR LEWIS**, FIRST AMERICAN RECIPIENT OF THE NOBEL PRIZE FOR LITERATURE

I cannot give the formula for success, but I can give you the formula of failure—which is to try to please everybody.

> —**HERBERT SWOPE**, FIRST PULITZER PRIZE WINNER FOR JOURNALISTIC REPORTING

I was ridiculed by journalists, businessmen, and even other scientists for believing that voice could ever be transmitted without using wires . . . . Not only was I wealthy from my patents, all of those people who had laughed at my ideas were twisting the dials on their newly bought radios to hear the latest weather and news.

> —**REGINALD FESSENDEN**, FIRST PERSON TO BROADCAST WORDS AND MUSIC OVER THE RADIO

We had only one thought: profound gratitude for the success achieved, gratitude toward all those who had contributed to the success of this uncommon day.

> —**JACQUES PICCARD**, OCEANOGRAPHER AND FIRST MAN TO REACH THE DEEPEST POINT ON THE EARTH IN THE PACIFIC OCEAN

It is clear now that the trek from Ward Hunt to the North Pole is never easy. It is, I am sure, the toughest trek on the planet. Even if you try to make something easier, such as having a re-supply, the Arctic Ocean is so varied and unpredictable that the trek is still a very hard journey.

—**RICHARD WEBER**, EXPLORER WHO POINEERED COMMERCIAL NORTH POLE EXPEDITIONS

I think nature tricks us a little bit because you tend to remember the good moments rather than the uncomfortable ones. So when you leave the mountain, you remember the great moments on the mountain, and as soon as you leave the mountain, you want to go back again.

—**SIR EDMUND HILLARY**, PART OF THE FIRST TEAM TO SUMMIT MOUNT EVEREST

You're all beautiful and you're all geniuses.

—**JOHN LENNON**, LEGENDARY MEMBER OF THE BEATLES AND FIRST PERSON TO APPEAR ON THE COVER OF *ROLLING STONE*

I'm not super anything. Maybe that's why people are personally interested in me, because I'm really pretty close to normal.

—**STEVE FOSSETT**, FIRST MAN TO FLY SOLO NONSTOP AROUND THE WORLD IN A BALLOON

Creating a nation requires the will of the people!

—**EDMUND BARTON**, FIRST PRIME MINISTER OF AUSTRALIA

It was certainly the ride of my life.

—**DENNIS TITO**, MULTIMILLIONAIRE AND FIRST SPACE TOURIST

Any coward can sit in his home and criticize a pilot for flying into a mountain in a fog. But I would rather, by far, die on a mountainside than in bed.

—**CHARLES LINDBERGH**, FIRST PERSON TO COMPLETE A SOLO TRANSATLANTIC FLIGHT

I like writing, although it's sometimes way more challenging than climbing.

—**ERIK WEIHENMAYER**, FIRST BLIND MAN TO
REACH THE SUMMIT OF MOUNT EVEREST

It's like going into battle. I have to get myself really
revved up, seriously aggressive. I dive in, and there's
only one place I'm getting out—and that's at the end.

—**LEWIS GORDON PUGH**, FIRST MAN TO
LONG-DISTANCE SWIM IN FIVE OCEANS

Where people of goodwill get together and transcend
their differences for the common good, peaceful and
just solutions can be found, even for those problems
that seem most intractable.

—**NELSON MANDELA**, CIVIL RIGHTS LEADER
AND FIRST BLACK MAN TO BE PRESIDENT
OF SOUTH AFRICA

Anybody who sees me skate, or golf, knows that I work best when I am surrounded by distraction, distraction, distraction. Of course those things have to be positive. When I warm up for a competition, sometimes I spend more time in the audience than I do actually skating.

—**KURT BROWNING**, FIRST SKATER TO DO A
QUADRUPLE JUMP IN A COMPETITION

People who say they don't care what people think are usually desperate to have people think they don't care what people think.

—**GEORGE CARLIN**, FIRST HOST OF
SATURDAY NIGHT LIVE

I enjoy the victory of it, but it's pure pain. I don't know anything about a zone, or getting into a flow. It's constant intensity and concentration. Nothing's flowing. You squeeze a joystick in your hand for hours and it starts to feel like it's going to shatter your hand.

—**BILLY MITCHELL**, FIRST PLAYER TO SCORE
A PERFECT GAME AT PACMAN

You miss 100 percent of the shots you never take.

—**WAYNE GRETZKY**, FIRST HOCKEY PLAYER
TO HAVE HIS NUMBER RETIRED

We must adhere staunchly to the basic principle that anything less than full equality is not enough. If we compromise on that principle our soul is dead.

—**RALPH BUNCHE**, FIRST BLACK MAN TO
RECEIVE THE NOBEL PEACE PRIZE

It was just an idea that I had, and I started it as an experiment, as a side hobby basically, while I had my day job. And it just kind of grew. Within six months, it was earning revenue that was paying my costs. Within nine months, the revenue was more than I was making on my day job, and that's kind of when the light bulb went off.

—**PIERRE OMIDYAR**, EBAY FOUNDER

When it was over, I was so happy I felt like crying.

—**DON LARSEN**, FIRST PITCHER TO PITCH A
PERFECT GAME IN A WORLD SERIES

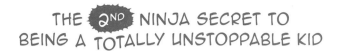

THE 2ND NINJA SECRET TO
BEING A TOTALLY UNSTOPPABLE KID

HOW TO BE
THE REAL DEAL
(REALISTIC EXPECTATIONS)

You're alone, standing in front of the TV. You close your eyes, wail on your guitar, and thrash your head around. You are a megastar—at Guitar Hero. Now pick up a real guitar and try the same song. Doesn't quite sound the same, does it?

The world's best guitar players practiced for years. They put a lot of time and energy into their music. Being really good at something—whether it's school, sports, or art—takes time, practice, and commitment.

It's true there are people who have natural talent, but even they dedicate themselves to getting better through practice. Shaun White was born with tremendous athletic talent. But he didn't become the world's most famous snowboarder by watching TV with his hand stuffed in a bag of potato chips. He practiced, practiced, practiced. And then he practiced some more.

Think of it this way: Don't expect to score an A on a report if you cranked it out the night before it's due. Good grades come from paying attention in class, planning ahead, and studying. Don't expect to run a 4-minute mile in your school's Presidential Fitness Test if you don't run or jog regularly—it takes a while to build up your endurance. Don't expect to beat your uncle at chess when you just learned to play. Chances are, he's been playing for years. You've got some catching up to do.

It's important to set goals and dream of success, as long as you recognize you've got to commit energy and effort. So set your expectations high—and don't trick yourself into thinking that you don't have to climb to reach them. ●

By no means in this world can you ever live up to someone else's expectations of who you are.

—**MICHAEL JORDAN**, LEGENDARY FORMER BASKETBALL PLAYER FOR THE CHICAGO BULLS

When in doubt, bail out. That's a good strategy on Everest and on smaller mountains. There's no loss of face or ego in turning around; it's just good judgment. If it doesn't look right today, it might tomorrow. Give yourself the opportunity to try in better conditions, rather than force your way up in dangerous conditions.

—**LOU WHITTAKER**, MOUNTAIN CLIMBER

When nobody around you seems to measure up, it's time to check your yardstick.

—**BILL LEMLEY**, WRITER

We set up harsh and unkind rules against ourselves. No one is born without faults. That man is best who has the fewest.

—**HORACE**, ROMAN POET

Putting off an easy thing makes it hard. Putting off a hard thing makes it impossible.

> —**GEORGE CLAUDE LORIMER**, MINISTER

You can't base your life on other people's expectations.

> —**STEVIE WONDER**, AWARD-WINNING BLIND
> SINGER AND SONGWRITER

I have tried to retain a balanced perspective about all that has occurred. I am still me. My family and my work helps me stay grounded.

> —**CHRISTOPHER PAOLINI**, FANTASY WRITER

We cannot all be masters.

> —**WILLIAM SHAKESPEARE**, ENGLISH
> PLAYWRIGHT

I hope to work, support my children, and die quietly without pain.

> —**SEAN CONNERY**, FIRST ACTOR TO PLAY
> JAMES BOND

Fame is a dirty game.

> —**SNOOP DOGG**, RECORD PRODUCER, ACTOR,
> AND AWARD-WINNING MUSICIAN

Life is a compromise of what your ego wants to do,
what your experience tells you to do, and what your
nerves let you do.

> —**BRUCE CRAMPTON**, AUSTRALIAN
> PROFESSIONAL GOLFER

You know you're not going to have a game every
night where offensively you're in tune. It doesn't
happen.

> —**LEBRON JAMES**, BASKETBALL PLAYER AND
> TWO-TIME NBA ALL-STAR MVP

With every preseason game I've played in, I'd love to
play the whole game. If I'm going to come out here
and practice, I'd love to play the whole game. That's
just my mentality. Will that happen? No. We're going
to be smart about it.

> —**BRETT FAVRE**, FOOTBALL PLAYER AND
> THREE-TIME NFL MVP

The good old days weren't so good when you were sitting in a dentist's chair.

> —**BOBBY BOWDEN**, COLLEGE FOOTBALL COACH

When one's expectations are reduced to zero, one really appreciates everything one does have.

> —**STEPHEN HAWKING**, AWARD-WINNING THEORETICAL PHYSICIST AND MATHEMATICIAN

Life didn't promise to be wonderful.

> —**TEDDY PENDERGRASS**, R&B/SOUL SINGER AND SONGWRITER

You got to be careful if you don't know where you're going, because you might not get there.

> —**YOGI BERRA**, FORMER MAJOR LEAGUE BASEBALL PLAYER AND MANAGER

He who wants to do everything will never do anything.

> —**ANDRES MAUROIS**, FRENCH WRITER

I'm not in this world to live up to your expectations and you're not in this world to live up to mine.

—**BRUCE LEE**, LEGENDARY MARTIAL ARTIST, ACTOR, AND FOUNDER OF JEET KUNE DO COMBAT

We always overestimate the change that will occur in the next two years and underestimate the change that will occur in the next ten. Don't let yourself be lulled into inaction.

—**BILL GATES**, FOUNDER OF MICROSOFT, MULTIBILLIONAIRE, AND PHILANTHROPIST

More and more it's about choosing your battles. Which ones are worth it. Which ones aren't worth it. And how much punishment can you take.

—**CHRIS COLE**, SKATEBOARDER AND *THRASHER* MAGAZINE 2005 SKATER OF THE YEAR

High achievement always takes place in the framework of high expectation.

—**JACK KINDER**, MANAGEMENT CONSULTANT

THE 3RD NINJA SECRET TO BEING A TOTALLY UNSTOPPABLE KID

HOW TO DEFEAT YOUR #1 ENEMY

(OVERCOMING NEGATIVITY)

Negativity is worst enemy when it comes to getting what you want out of life. Consider this:

You assume the coolest girl in class doesn't like you. So what happens? You don't say hi, you don't smile, and you don't even look at her when she arrives in the morning. And she thinks, "He's kind of a jerk." You've cemented your own image.

You dread an upcoming visit with your cousins. You think about how they whine and mess up your stuff. When they get there, all you do is listen for whining instead of noticing how much they admire you.

You're positive your soccer team is going to blow the next game. You complain to your teammates and you don't sleep well because you're thinking about the tough opposing team. The result: You're too tired to play well and your teammates don't have the confidence to do their best.

Some people seem to feed on negativity's dark energy. You probably know some of them. They're always hating on other people. They always assume the worst and they constantly point out what's wrong. Having strep throat is more fun than hanging out with them.

But if *you're* the one with the bad attitude, maybe it's time to go on hate-cation. Taking a break from negativity just might change your life. You could become friends with the cool girl, have fun with your cousins, and your team might just win the game. ●

We are capable of freaking ourselves out way beyond comprehension, whereas the world is a little more gentle on us than we are on ourselves sometimes.

—JOHN KRASINSKI, ACTOR WHO APPEARED IN THE OFFICE

You have to believe in happiness or happiness never comes.

—DOUGLAS MALLOCH, POET

There are a lot of things that are wrong with the world, but if you watch the news, that's not the world; that's a condensed version of everything negative that's happening. If I look around the television set, things are pretty peaceful, and people treat each other pretty well.

—JIM CARREY, AWARD-WINNING FILM ACTOR AND COMEDIAN

Attitudes are contagious. Are yours worth catching?

—DENNIS AND WENDY MANNERING, CORPORATE TRAINERS

I'll come to an intersection and mess up, but then I have to turn around and go back.

—**PAUL MAURICE**, NATIONAL HOCKEY
LEAGUE COACH

The more fun I'm having, the better I do.

—**ERIC JACKSON**, FREESTYLE KAYAK
CHAMPION

I don't live angrily. I don't live with hate. I don't have any grudges in life. I've never held grudges. I've never had resentment. I see people who have that and I think, "What a waste of time." I've really never been in a fight.

—**GEORGE CARLIN**, AWARD-WINNING
COMEDIAN AND WRITER

It's like ballplayers. You can't get too upset if you lose two or three games in a row because, good Lord, you're playing 162.

—**DAVID LETTERMAN**, TALK SHOW HOST
AND COMEDIAN

If you keep on saying things are going to be bad, you have a good chance of being a prophet.

> —ISAAC BASHEVIS SINGER, WRITER AND
> RECIPIENT OF NOBEL PRIZE

A happy person is not a person in a certain set of circumstances, but rather a person with a certain set of attitudes.

> —HUGH DOWNS, JOURNALIST AND RETIRED
> ANCHOR OF 20/20 AND HOST OF THE
> TODAY SHOW

Optimism is the foundation of courage.

> —NICHOLAS MURRAY BUTLER,
> PHILOSOPHER, EDUCATOR, AND RECIPIENT
> OF NOBEL PRIZE

Most of the important things in the world have been accomplished by people who have kept on trying when there seemed to be no hope at all.

> —DALE CARNEGIE, ENTREPRENEUR AND
> WRITER KNOWN FOR HOW TO WIN FRIENDS
> AND INFLUENECE PEOPLE

I don't think I'm really in a situation to complain. I consider myself to be privileged to be doing what I do.

—**DAVID BECKHAM**, SOCCER PLAYER

Sometimes we stare so long at a door that is closing that we see too late the one that is open.

—**ALEXANDER GRAHAM BELL**, INVENTOR
   KNOWN FOR INVENTING THE TELEPHONE

The greatest discovery of my generation is that man can alter his life simply by altering his attitude of mind.

—**WILLIAM JAMES**, PHILOSOPHER AND
   BROTHER OF NOVELIST HENRY JAMES

For a lot of people, [getting Parkinson's disease] is like being hit by a truck. But in a way it's also gift—one that keeps on taking, but still a gift. To be able to be of service, to help people—that's the greatest privilege I could have.

—**MICHAEL J. FOX**, ACTOR FAMOUS FOR
   ROLES IN *FAMILY TIES* AND *BACK TO THE
   FUTURE*

Ability is what you're capable of doing. Motivation determines what you do. Attitude determines how well you do it.

> —**LOU HOLTZ,** FORMER NCAA FOOTBALL
> PLAYER AND NFL HEAD COACH

I don't believe in pessimism.

> —**CLINT EASTWOOD,** AWARD-WINNING
> ACTOR, DIRECTOR, AND ANTI-HERO

Hope is a good thing, maybe the best of things, and no good thing ever dies.

> —**STEPHEN KING,** HORROR FICTION WRITER
> KNOWN FOR *CARRIE*, *CUJO*, AND *THE
> SHINING*

I've always tried to learn something. I look at the work as a learning experience so I never see anything as a waste of time.

> —**JUDD APATOW,** AWARD-WINNING
> SCREENWRITER AND DIRECTOR KNOWN
> FOR *KNOCKED UP* AND *SUPERBAD*

HOW TO OPEN DOORS
WITH A MAGIC WORD

(BEING THANKFUL)

It's easy to be thankful on your birthday when there's a pile of presents on the floor and your best buddies are spending the night. But on other days, being thankful can seem harder than biting into a frozen jawbreaker. When you look around and see that your friends have more things than you do, it's tough to feel grateful. That's because you've let your mind focus on what's *not* in your life.

Your mind is yours to control. That means you have the ability to change your focus. If you're having trouble feeling or showing gratitude, try these tricks:

Make a list of what makes you happy. It seems strange, but the actual act of writing can make the good things in your life seem a little more "real."

Take that list and stick it under your pillow. Read it every night when you crawl into bed. The list becomes a launch pad for expressing gratitude for your everything you have. And clearing your mind of bummer thoughts is a surefire way to fall asleep.

Ask your parents and grandparents what they're thankful for—you're probably at the top of their list! Most likely, there aren't a lot of *things* on their list. They'll probably tell you they're grateful for friends and family, good health, their home, their faith, and other things that aren't necessarily bought and sold.

It's not always easy to change your focus. If your little sister just spilled orange juice on your Wii, you're probably not in the mood to make a list of the good things in your life. But when it comes to getting what you want out of life, "thanks" is a magic word that can open a lot of doors.●

When I started counting my blessings, my whole life turned around.

—**WILLIE NELSON**, COUNTRY MUSIC SINGER

I happen to think that the great spirit God made us all, put us all here for a reason. And all of us have something to do.

—**B. B. KING**, BLUES GUITARIST AND SINGER SONGWRITER

There's a lot of goodwill out there for what I've done. And I didn't really appreciate it so much before. I really appreciate it now.

—**BILL MURRAY**, ACTOR KNOWN FOR ROLES IN *SATURDAY NIGHT LIVE* AND *GHOSTBUSTERS*

I was born in a council house, which is government housing, in North London. And I grew up in my grandmother's house. And so to have the life that I've had and to end up being a knight or a sir, it makes me very proud.

—**ELTON JOHN**, SINGER SONGWRITER, COMPOSER, AND PIANIST

I like the way I am. And I like the way I've ended up. I'm very happy right now. If I changed one little thing I wouldn't be the person I am today.

—**MACAULAY CULKIN**, ACTOR AND STAR OF
   HOME ALONE

We've been doing this awhile, obviously, and now you look out in the crowd and you've got like, probably a 30-year-old dad or something who's got his 7 or 10-year-old son on his shoulders, with the horns up going, yes! You're like, wow, this is crazy. It's cool.

—**TOMMY LEE**, MUSICIAN AND FOUNDING
   MEMBER OF MÖTLEY CRÜE

After you span 20 years, then you can start talking to me about having a career. I've gone over that cliff now, and I'm in the 24th year of my recording career. Yes, we have been up and we have been down, but this is one of the up years, and it feels good.

—**JON BON JOVI**, MUSICIAN AND
   SONGWRITER

Why do some people always see beautiful skies and grass and lovely flowers and incredible human beings, while others are hard-pressed to find anything or any place that is beautiful?

—**LEO BUSCAGLIA**, WRITER, PROFESSOR, AND MOTIVATIONAL SPEAKER

There is a calmness of life lived in Gratitude, a quiet joy.

—**RALPH H. BLUM**, WRITER AND CULTURAL ANTHROPOLOGIST

It's not a nuisance when somebody comes up to me on the street and says, "Hey, I was having kind of a bad time, and I went to one of your movies, and it really took my mind off of it for a couple of hours." It's a really great feeling.

—**BEN STILLER**, AWARD-WINNING ACTOR AND STAR OF *ZOOLANDER*

Somehow, through some odd twist of fate, I became an actor. Somewhere throughout that process, I fell in love with acting. I love acting. To me, it's the same thing as making music. It's just being real.

—BILLY RAY CYRUS, AWARD-WINNING COUNTRY MUSIC SINGER AND ACTOR

I got lucky and ended up in a situation where I'm able to express myself. A lot of people want to do creative work but never get a job where somebody lets them do it. I got really lucky, and then I was very aggressive about trying to make the most of it.

—IRA GLASS, RADIO HOST AND PRODUCER OF *THIS AMERICAN LIFE*

When I see someone without basic health and education, without a supportive family, I feel a connection. That's what moves me the most. I could be him, if I'd been born on some other dot on the map.

—BRAD PITT, AWARD-WINNING ACTOR AND PRODUCER

Feeling gratitude and not expressing it is like wrapping a present and not giving it.

—**WILLIAM ARTHUR WARD**, INSPIRATIONAL WRITER

When I first open my eyes upon the morning meadows, and look out upon the beautiful world, I thank God I am alive.

—**RALPH WALDO EMERSON**, PHILOSOPHER AND POET

You change as you go. Time alters you. It's been a flip from the time when I was a shy, unhappy teenager. Now I can appreciate my own joy and my sense of irony.

—**DUSTIN HOFFMAN**, AWARD-WINNING ACTOR KNOWN FOR ROLES SUCH AS *RAIN MAN*

The hardest arithmetic to master is that which enables us to count our blessings.

—**ERIC HOFFER**, WRITER AND PHILOSOPHER

The advantages of a losing team: 1.) There is every-thing to hope for and nothing to fear. 2.) Defeats do not disturb one's sleep. 3.) An occasional victory is a surprise and a delight. 4.) There is no danger of any club passing you. 5.) You are not asked fifty times a day, "What was the score." People take it for granted that you lost.

—**ELMER E. BATES**, SPORTS WRITER

Too many people miss the silver lining because they're expecting gold.

—**MAURICE SETTER**, SOCCER PLAYER AND MANAGER

If you count all your assets, you always show a profit.

—**ROBERT QUILLEN**, JOURNALIST AND HUMORIST

May we never let the things we can't have or don't have spoil our enjoyment of the things we do have and can have.

—**RICHARD L. EVANS**, MINISTER

One of my most interesting experiences in the mountains had nothing to do with climbing. I crested a small hill and found myself face-to-face with a snow leopard. It was an incredible experience, and it shows how the good times had while climbing have as much to do with the places you go and people you go with as with the actual climbing.

—JOHN ROSKELLEY, MOUNTAIN CLIMBER

Some people are always grumbling because roses have thorns; I am thankful that thorns have roses.

—JEAN-BAPTISTE ALPHONSE KARR, FRENCH JOURNALIST AND NOVELIST

Knowing that I don't have control over things is not always exciting for me, but it's been reassuring to know that I don't need to have control. God has control.

—CLAY AIKEN, SINGER DISCOVERED ON *AMERICAN IDOL*

THE 5TH NINJA SECRET TO
BEING A TOTALLY UNSTOPPABLE KID

LIVING THE LIFE
OF A WANTED MAN

(FEELING NEEDED)

Sometimes you might feel like you're nothing but one big hassle. Who's going to pick you up from soccer practice? Who's going to make dinner for you? Who's going to your school's parent–teacher conference? It can make you feel like you're just another chore—like getting the groceries or doing the laundry.

But you are *not* a chore. People need you—especially your parents. Adults thrive when they have their children's time and affection. That's why they sometimes embarrass you by hugging you in front of your friends.

Other adults need you, too. Grandparents, aunts, and uncles need to share their wisdom with younger generations. Telling you their stories and giving advice helps them feel needed and important. Even your teachers need you. They studied for years to be teachers, and they need kids who are eager to learn from them. That's what makes their job fun and rewarding.

Kids need you, too. Maybe you're the alpha dog in a litter of brothers and sisters, or maybe you're the ringleader of that circus of kids in your neighborhood. Think about your possible list of admirers: the little kids down the block, your younger cousins, and the kids in lower grades at school. Maybe you haven't been paying attention, but if you start watching, you'll see they look up to you. They ask you a lot of questions, follow you around, and maybe even copy what you do. You've probably been thinking they were pests, but they're actually your own little fan club.

So whenever you're feeling like a chore, think of your school picture as a wanted poster. Because people want—and need—you. ●

I don't believe in hiding things. A lot of people want to hide things and not let people know the truth because they feel that there's a kind of control or power in that. See, I believe the opposite. If I've done something and it's helped me, I'll turn to anyone and say, "Look, I've gone *this* way."

—**TOM CRUISE**, STAR OF THE *MISSION IMPOSSIBLE* MOVIES

A man wrapped up in himself makes a very small bundle.

—**BENJAMIN FRANKLIN**, INVENTOR, STATESMAN, AND U.S. FOUNDING FATHER

Man absolutely cannot live by himself.

—**ERICH FROMM**, PHILOSOPHER AND PSYCHOLOGIST

Success has nothing to do with what you gain in life or accomplish for yourself. It's what you do for others.

—**DANNY THOMAS**, ACTOR AND COMEDIAN

The golden rule is of no use whatsoever unless you realize that it is your move.

—**FRANK CRANE**, AUTHOR AND MINISTER

Time and money spent in helping men to do more for themselves is far better than mere giving.

—**HENRY FORD**, FOUNDER OF FORD MOTOR COMPANY

In poverty and other misfortunes of life, true friends are a sure refuge.

—**ARISTOTLE**, GREEK PHILOSOPHER

Pretty much all the honest truth telling there is in the world is done by children.

—**OLIVER WENDELL HOLMES**, PHYSICIAN AND POET

I allow my curiosity and enthusiasm for learning to match my students.

—**MICHAEL GEISEN**, 2008 NATIONAL TEACHER OF THE YEAR

In about the same degree as you are helpful, you will be happy.

—**KARL REILAND**, MINISTER

All the years that I was teaching I was learning. That was the main thing in my life, I think. I became a human being in front of those classes.

—**FRANK MCCOURT**, TEACHER AND WRITER
    BEST KNOWN FOR HIS MEMOIR *ANGELA'S
    ASHES*

How pleasant it is for a father to sit at his child's board. It is like an aged man reclining under the shadow of an oak which he has planted.

—**WALTER SCOTT**, WRITER

There's the old saying, "Adults don't make kids. Kids make adults." And I firmly believe that. When you have a kid, it's like a whole other world opens up, and it's pretty amazing.

—**ROB ESTES**, ACTOR FIRST SEEN ON *DAYS OF
    OUR LIVES*

Brothers don't necessarily have to say anything to each other—they can sit in a room and be together and just be completely comfortable with each other.

—**LEONARDO DICAPRIO**, ACTOR KNOWN FOR ROLES IN *TITANIC* AND *ROMEO & JULIET*

Grief can take care of itself, but to get the full value of joy you must have somebody to divide it with.

—**MARK TWAIN**, HUMORIST AND WRITER

When friends stop being frank and useful to each other, the whole world loses some of its radiance.

—**ANATOLE BROYARD**, LITERARY CRITIC FOR *THE NEW YORK TIMES*

My mother is my hero. She once told me, "If you can't give 110 percent, you won't make it," and I've never forgotten that. She is my best friend, my motivator, and my most loyal ally. I wish everyone had at least one person who inspires him or her the way my mother inspires me.

—**LANCE ARMSTRONG**, CYCLIST AND SEVEN-TIME WINNER OF THE TOUR DE FRANCE

Seeing my kids succeed and be happy is the best thing in life.

—**SAL PACINO**, BUSINESSMAN AND FATHER OF ACTOR AL PACINO

The highlight of my childhood was making my brother laugh so hard that food came out his nose.

—**GARRISON KEILLOR**, WRITER AND RADIO HOST OF *A PRAIRIE HOME COMPANION*

The thing that amazes me is that you can watch a baby like a TV set for hours at a time. "Oh my God, he moved!" It's the greatest thing in the world.

—**HAROLD RAMIS**, DIRECTOR AND ACTOR BEST KNOWN FOR ROLE IN *GHOSTBUSTERS*

I figure somewhere between kid number one and number seven, I must have learned a few things.

—**MEL GIBSON**, ACTOR AND DIRECTOR OF THE AWARD-WINNING MOVIE *BRAVEHEART*

THE 6TH NINJA SECRET TO
BEING A TOTALLY UNSTOPPABLE KID

HOW TO FIND AND KEEP
A TRUSTY SIDEKICK

(FRIENDSHIP)

Are you the kind of guy who likes to hang out with one favorite buddy? Or do you like to surround yourself with all kinds of people—funny guys, athletic guys, musical guys, motorsports guys and, once in a while, a cool girl? No matter which kind of person you are, you probably agree there's nothing like a good pal.

But it's one thing to *say* somebody is your friend. It's another thing to *act* like a good friend in return. Here are some ways to always be a winner in the friendship game:

Never say anything about a buddy that you wouldn't say to his face. That way you'll never have to keep track of lies, and you won't get in the habit of saying things that tick him off.

Meeting new people is fun, but don't forget your old crew. There's an old saying that new friends are silver, but old friends are gold. (And gold is one of the most valuable metals on the planet!)

Let a friend know you care about him. You don't have to write him a lame poem or act sappy. You can show a buddy what you think and feel by giving him something important to you, like a favorite baseball card, telling him how funny he is, or high-fiving him when he does something great.

When you were little, your friends were chosen for you. Your parents set up play dates and you didn't have contact with kids other than those in your neighborhood or day care. Now it's different. You're choosing your own friends, and that comes with the responsibility of *being* a friend.●

It is rarely the destination or type of job that excites me. It is the people I work with and new people I meet that make what I do so enjoyable. The people make the place, so I try hard to surround myself with like minds and good people.

> —NIGEL BARKER, BRITISH FASHION PHOTOGRAPHER

I had dear friends, and you know they're your friends because they can listen to you say the same thing over and over again.

> —ALEC BALDWIN, AWARD-WINNING FILM ACTOR

A friend is, as it were, a second self.

> —CICERO, ROMAN PHILOSOPHER

Any time I have some of my friends come out, whether it's Eva Longoria or George Lopez, it's going to be fun. I love having my friends on the set because it's always fun just messing around.

> —MARIO LOPEZ, TELEVISION HOST AND ACTOR KNOWN FOR ROLE IN *SAVED BY THE BELL*

A friend of mine once sent me a postcard with a picture of the entire planet Earth taken from space. On the back it said, "Wish you were here."

—**STEVEN WRIGHT**, AWARD-WINNING COMEDIAN

If someone would harm my family or my friend or somebody I love, I would eat them. I might spend 500 years in jail, but I would eat them.

—**JOHNNY DEPP**, AWARD-WINNING ACTOR STARRING IN *EDWARD SCISSORHANDS* AND *PIRATES OF THE CARIBBEAN*

I'm now aware of how brief life is and how you have to mark every day and make it matter—not just the best moments, the award nominations, the opening nights. If all my life is about is these satellite moments, what then? They come, and they're gone. I have to live it whole. It's finally about friendship and loyalty and treating people right.

—**GEORGE CLOONEY**, AWARD-WINNING ACTOR KNOWN FOR *ER* AND *OCEAN'S ELEVEN*

There is nothing on this earth more to be prized than true friendship.

—SAINT THOMAS AQUINAS, THEOLOGIAN
AND PHILOSOPHER

Sometimes if you're lucky, someone comes into your life who'll take up a place in your heart that no one else can fill, someone who's tighter than a twin, more with you than your own shadow, who gets deeper under your skin than your own blood and bones.

—SNOOP DOGG, RECORD PRODUCER, ACTOR,
AND AWARD-WINNING MUSICIAN

Neither of us really long to be screenwriters, but at the same time, that would be a category in which we'd be nominated together. I don't care if we were nominated for Best Morons, because I'd think, Well, I got nominated with Ben [Affleck], and that's pretty cool . . . . If you put us together, you might actually make a whole, creative, interesting individual. We're a lot like the Wonder Twins.

—MATT DAMON, AWARD-WINNING ACTOR
AND CO-STAR IN GOOD WILL HUNTING

Most of your male friendships are kind of marriages without sex. Most times you meet a lot of guys who'd much rather hang out with their friends than with their wives or girlfriends. There's a reason for that. When men bond, they bond hard.

—**KEVIN SMITH**, DIRECTOR AND COMIC
BOOK WRITER

True friendship is like sound health; the value of it is seldom known until it be lost.

—**CHARLES CALEB COLTON**, WRITER AND
ART COLLECTOR

A true friend is one who overlooks your failures and tolerates your success!

—**DOUG LARSON**, COLUMNIST

No man is wise enough by himself.

—**PLAUTUS**, ROMAN PLAYWRIGHT

The best way to keep your friends is not to give them away.

—**WILSON MIZNER**, PLAYWRIGHT

Friendship is the only cement that will ever hold the world together.

—**WOODROW WILSON**, 28TH PRESIDENT OF
THE UNITED STATES

Each one of us has, at one time or another, stepped out to protect not only our own interests but the interests of the band. It's rare to be with the same people 35 or 40 years after you started with them, and at this point in our lives, its pleasures are very great. You really appreciate the guy next to you, you know?

—**BRUCE SPRINGSTEEN**, MUSICIAN AND
FRONTMAN FOR THE E STREET BAND

The only way to have a friend is to be one.

—**RALPH WALDO EMERSON**, PHILOSOPHER
AND POET

Lead the life that will make you kindly and friendly to everyone about you, and you will be surprised what a happy life you will live.

—**CHARLES SCHWAB**, BUSINESSMAN

THE 7TH NINJA SECRET TO BEING A TOTALLY UNSTOPPABLE KID

HOW TO FIND THE ULTIMATE MASK OR COSTUME

(SELF-DISCOVERY)

When you were a little squirt, did you ever spend hours and hours trying to figure out what you wanted to be for Halloween? You'd try on all kinds of lame clown or pirate outfits—or expensive rubber masks that smelled like other people's stinky breath—when suddenly, it dawned on you: "I've got it—I'll go as The Joker!"

It's no joke to say that life is a lot like choosing Halloween costumes. The only way you'll ever find out what role you were meant to play is try different things. Think you're born to be a drummer? A game designer? A rock climber? It's important to experiment with a bunch of

57

activities and hobbies to learn what you're good at—and what you like. You don't want to spend all your time doing one thing and figure out later that you missed a lot of fun.

You'll have to commit some time to those activities, too. Rock climbers spend years building strong bodies and learning how to safely maneuver through dangerous terrain. Video game designers study math and computer science in school, and drummers practice, practice, practice.

The game designer probably didn't have a clue what his job would be when he was a kid. He may have played soccer, joined a church youth group, and earned a purple belt in karate. Chances are he didn't lay in bed at night dreaming up computer code. He tried a lot of things as a kid and figured it out as he got older.

Ever heard adults talk about how they had to "find themselves" when they were younger? Well, ready or not, you're about to go on the same adventure.●

I don't remember when it happened, but it didn't take long for me to realize that I wanted to become a full-time skater. I try to skate every day, but even on the days when I don't, I know that I am still a skater from the time I wake up to the time I go to sleep. Skating is my life.

—**AARON FEINBERG**, STREET SKATER

I've been approached occasionally about doing dance-music records. I have no taste whatsoever for dance music—it means nothing to me. And for me to work on a record like that, just for a paycheck, would be crass and insincere and dishonest.

—**STEVE ALBINI**, RECORD PRODUCER

Writing is the finest and most important and most rewarding of all vocations except for the part where you have to buy food. So by all means, write on. But don't say I didn't warn you.

—**PETE HAUTMAN**, WRITER

As a kid, I liked being in the kitchen, cooking with my mom. I remember watching all the cooking shows—with the Galloping Gourmet, Julia Child—instead of cartoons.

—**STEVE ELLS**, FOUNDER OF CHIPOTLE

You want to justify the resources you're taking up, and writing is the only way I know to do that. It's wonderful to find one's own niche.

—**JOHN UPDIKE**, WRITER

As soon as you trust yourself, you will know how to live.

—**JOHANN VON GOETHE**, GERMAN WRITER

Even in the toughest times, it's still fun. I'd play football all my life if I could. There's really not a time when football is not fun.

—**ED REED**, FOOTBALL PLAYER

If you are going to doubt something, doubt your limits.

—**DON WARD**, ARTIST

When I'm doing distance stuff, it feels like that's what I was born to do. I absolutely love it. I don't get nervous, I just have a blast. It's hard to even put into words.

—PAUL THACKER, SNOWMOBILER

The thing always happens that you really believe in; and the belief in a thing makes it happen.

—FRANK LLOYD WRIGHT, ARCHITECT

Immediately, I saw that we were a rock 'n roll *brand*, not just a rock 'n roll band. See, the rest of the guys with guitars around their necks want credibility. I don't want credibility. That means nothing.

—GENE SIMMONS, MUSICIAN

I've always had such a passion for skiing, but haven't and still really don't take it that seriously. What keeps me hiking all day, lapping the park from 9-4, or hitting the same handrail 80 times is simply my love of the sport itself. I would never consider any day of skiing "training" or anything like that.

—TOM WALLISCH, SKIER

It's a great time to be in the commentary business. You get more feedback, more people screaming at you, blogging with you, blogging against you. It's the most fun you can have legally that I know of.

>—**THOMAS FRIEDMAN**, WRITER

At its core, I love playing baseball. That's why I'm here—the joy.

>—**SALVATORE FRANK FASANO**, BASEBALL
>PLAYER

If you think you can, you can. And if you think you can't, you're right.

>—**HENRY FORD**, FOUNDER OF FORD MOTOR
>COMPANY

When love and skill work together, expect a masterpiece.

>—**JOHN RUSKIN**, ART CRITIC

Give me a man who sings at his work.

>—**THOMAS CARLYLE**, WRITER AND
>HISTORIAN

Surfing big waves has always been part of my life. It's not a macho thing—it's pure passion for wave riding.

    —**TIMMY REYES**, SURFER

Experience tells you what to do; confidence allows you to do it.

    —**STAN SMITH**, TENNIS PLAYER

I've been directing movies since the early 70s. I've got twenty-some-odd movies. Not that I'm a talented director. I'm probably a footnote in history, but I'm a footnote that's influenced.

    —**LLOYD KAUFMAN**, FILM DIRECTOR

I make my money going fast. I love going fast. But I'm in the powder and the trees, too.

    —**JEFF HAMILTON**, SPEED SKIER

Whenever it is possible, a boy should choose some occupation which he should do even if he did not need the money.

    —**WILLIAM LYON PHELPS**, AUTHOR

SPARRING LESSONS

NOW... LOCK YOUR SWORD WITH MINE!

CHING!

TRY TO KNOCK ME OVER.

PUSH HARD!

I....I CAN'T!

SSSSHING

THUD...

UFF!

YOU'RE NOT A NINJA UNTIL YOU DO THE THINGS YOU THINK YOU CAN'T!

HOW TO DO
THE IMPOSSIBLE
(EXPANDING YOUR HORIZONS)

Has an adult ever told you that you can "be any-thing you want to be"? That may seem a little hard to believe some days. Let's face it, none of us are going to slay dragons in a magic kingdom no matter how hard we chase that dream.

But there is truth behind the dream-it, do-it concept. Your mind is a powerful force. Whether you want to ride in a hot-air balloon, ace a tough test, or catch a record-sized fish, the simple act of having a dream is the first step toward making it come true.

Dream big. Don't just try easy things because you'll know you'll succeed. Set the bar high for yourself. If you succeed, you'll feel great. And if you fall short of your goal, you'll still have done much more than you would have if you had taken the easy route.

Make a plan. Plans turn dreams into goals. Write down a list of all the steps you have to take to achieve your dream. Then tackle those steps one at a time. Breaking big dreams down into little steps will make them seem more doable.

Work every day at your plan. Don't expect overnight success. Just work on your plan diligently and consistently and you'll get a little closer to your dream each day!

Don't get discouraged. Sometimes a part of your plan won't work. Don't lose hope—sit down again and rewrite that step or the next few steps until you can get back on track.

There's nothing like taking a few minutes to stare out a window and let your mind become a movie screen, playing out your dreams vividly and in high definition.●

I see so many people today that don't want to try,
and I say, "I don't care what I ever do, I never give up
at anything anymore." I don't care what it is, you'll
never see me give up.

—**HERSCHEL WALKER**, FOOTBALL PLAYER

My greatest point is my perseverance. I never give up
in a match. However down I am, I fight until the last
ball.

—**BJORN BORG**, ACCLAIMED TENNIS PLAYER

Every noble work is at first impossible.

—**THOMAS CARLYLE**, HISTORIAN AND
WRITER

My motivation can be a totally different thing on any
given day. The sport constantly changes. Everything
changes—the bikes, the ramps, the trends, and
sometimes riding even takes a step backwards. The
sport is always changing, and from that standpoint,
you can't help but stay motivated. I guess it really
comes down to the love of riding.

—**DENNIS MCCOY**, CYCLIST

I was pretty ambitious. I felt like I had a good imagination and vision for my life. And I had people telling me "You are driving the vehicle of your life here. You are the master of your own destiny in a sense. Do whatever you want to do."

—**TOBEY MAGUIRE**, ACTOR AND STAR OF
    SPIDER-MAN

I just try to push myself, even when I'm hurting or I fight getting up. Sometimes [the coaches] will put us through a practice that'll just kill you, your whole legs, everything just shuts down. I try to get up from that. I just work hard.

—**HENRY CEJUDO**, OLYMPIC WRESTLER

Man is what he believes.

—**ANTON CHEKHOV**, DOCTOR, WRITER, AND
    PLAYWRIGHT OF WORKS SUCH AS UNCLE
    VANYA

Do your best every day and your life will gradually expand into satisfying fullness.

—**HORATIO W. DRESSER**, PHILOSOPHER

My motivation was to get my family out of poverty. I wanted to be their hero, the first guy to help my family out.

— **TORII HUNTER**, BASEBALL PLAYER

Quality is not an act. It is a habit.

— **ARISTOTLE**, GREEK PHILOSOPHER

I'm not the biggest guy on the field, but you're going to have to do everything in your power to stop me.

— **REGGIE BUSH**, AWARD-WINNING FOOTBALL PLAYER

I never lost a game. I just ran out of time.

— **BOBBY LAYNE**, FOOTBALL PLAYER IN THE COLLEGE FOOTBALL HALL OF FAME

I'd grown up on a farm in Tennessee. The only real workouts I ever had were baling hay or mucking out stalls. Not that I planned on doing that for long. I had big dreams for myself, hopes that I could make a difference in the world.

— **BOB HARPER**, CELEBRITY FITNESS TRAINER

69

I don't believe in talking to them about things that they can't change. . . . Perhaps we need to acknowledge those limitations, but not dwell on them. Just accept them! Instead, let's look at what we can do and let's look together at where we can have the biggest impact.

—**TIM GUNN,** FASHION DESIGNER KNOWN
FOR ROLE ON *PROJECT RUNWAY*

I think and think for months and years. Ninety nine times, the conclusion is false. The hundredth time I am right.

—**ALBERT EINSTEIN,** PHYSICIST BEST KNOWN
FOR HIS THEORY OF RELATIVITY

I failed at many jobs when I was younger—like getting fired from a gas station because my handwriting was so bad no one could ever read what I wrote on charge slips. Now I look at setbacks as a sign that there is another, probably better opportunity elsewhere. I just need to find it!

—**PAUL ORFALEA,** BUSINESSMAN AND
FOUNDER OF KINKO'S

In order to be a fierce competitor, you have to have an incredible fire and desire and drive and be willing to make every possible sacrifice and compromise in your life to be able to get out there. That's what I've done and that's what I still do.

—**MARK MARTIN**, CAR RACER

Nobody who ever gave his best regretted it.

—**GEORGE HALAS**, FOUNDER OF THE
CHICAGO BEARS

Yesterday is a cancelled check. Tomorrow is a promissory note. Today is cash in hand. Spend it!

—**JOHN W. NEWBERN**, PHILOSOPHER

You're never a loser until you quit trying.

—**MIKE DITKA**, FOOTBALL COACH KNOWN
AS "IRON MIKE"

Clear your mind of "can't."

—**SAMUEL JOHNSON**, WRITER AND AUTHOR
OF *A DICTIONARY OF THE ENGLISH
LANGUAGE* (1755)

THE 9TH NINJA SECRET TO BEING A TOTALLY UNSTOPPABLE KID

WHY EVERY HERO HAS A SECRET HIDEOUT

(FINDING YOUR HAPPY PLACE)

For some guys, happiness is a day of hanging with their buddies. For others, bliss is smashing somebody else's high score on a video game.

But sometimes you're doing your favorite thing, and all of a sudden, you're annoyed. There's no good reason—you're just ticked off. Those might be your hormones on overdrive—and they'll jerk you around like that for a few years.

There's no miracle cure for roller coaster moods, but here are a few tips:

- Do something relaxing. Online RPGs or other video games may be a blast, but the competition and intensity may stress you out. Your shoulders tighten. Your hands get stiff and your vision starts to blur. That's some full-body stress! Try something more low key: read a graphic novel or go on a bike ride.

- Take a time out to think about good things: your friends, your favorite things to do, your favorite places to go. Thinking about the really killer things in your life can help you zone out whatever else is bugging you.

- Talk to your friends or to an adult you trust. Sometimes talking is like making a slow leak in a balloon: the tension slowly deflates. It's doubly important to talk to an adult if you feel like you feel like you're about to have a total meltdown.

There's a reason superheroes and supervillains have their secret caves and lairs: all guys need places and activities that helps them de-stress, defuse, and just plain "chillax" a little bit.

Being happy is something you have to learn. I often surprise myself by saying, "Wow, this is it. I guess I'm happy. I got a home I love. A career that I love. I'm even feeling more and more at peace with myself." If there's something else to happiness, let me know. I'm ambitious for that, too.

—**HARRISON FORD**, STAR OF THE *INDIANA JONES* MOVIES

Don't mistake pleasures for happiness. They are a different breed of dog.

—**JOSH BILLINGS**, PROFESSIONAL FUNNY GUY

I feel like everything in my life depends on physical conditioning. I love eating sweets and everything, but I think the quality of my parenting, the quality of my relationship with my wife—it is all based on being in great physical condition. I believe it's the beginning of finding true happiness.

—**WILL SMITH**, STAR OF THE MOVIES *HANCOCK* AND *I AM LEGEND*

Success is not the key to happiness. Happiness is the key to success. If you love what you are doing, you will be successful.

>—**ALBERT SCHWEITZER**, GERMAN
> PHILOSOPHER

All I can say about life is…enjoy it!

>—**BOB NEWHART**, ACTOR WHO PLAYED WILL
> FERRELL'S DAD IN *ELF*

The U.S. Constitution doesn't guarantee happiness, only the pursuit of it. You have to catch up with it yourself.

>—**BENJAMIN FRANKLIN**, INVENTOR AND U.S.
> STATESMAN

I'm happier—I guess I made up my mind to be that way.

>—**MERLE HAGGARD**, "OUTLAW" COUNTRY
> SINGER

I try not to get ahead of myself in terms of the next thing. I've been really lucky just to support myself acting and being able to help create and be the lead in a movie is way beyond any expectation I have had. I am pretty happy with what's happened so far. Honestly if this is it, and it crashes down tomorrow, I'm happy.

—STEVE CARELL, ACTOR IN *LITTLE MISS SUNSHINE* AND *GET SMART*

Seek to do good, and you will find that happiness will run after you.

—JAMES FREEMAN CLARKE, MINISTER AND WRITER

Anytime you're doing something you love that you're good at, the only thing you have to add to that is recognition for it, and you've got the package for success or happiness or whatever you want to call it. It's just so great!

—GEORGE CARLIN, COMEDIAN AND WRITER

Happiness sneaks in through a door you didn't know you left open.

> —**JOHN BARRYMORE**, ACTOR AND
> GRANDFATHER OF ACTRESS DREW
> BARRYMORE

The formula for complete happiness is to be very busy.

> —**EDWARD NEWTON**, SCIENTIST

I know a lot of people who have a lot of everything and they're absolutely the most miserable people in the world. So it won't do anything for you unless you're a happy person and can have peace with yourself.

> —**LENNY KRAVITZ**, AWARD-WINNING
> MUSICIAN AND RECORDING ARTIST

One of the things I keep learning is that the secret of being happy is doing things for other people.

> —**DICK GREGORY**, COMEDIAN, WRITER, AND
> ACTIVITIST

Fun is about as good of a habit as there is.

—**JIMMY BUFFETT**, SINGER AND SONGWRITER

Success can also cause misery. The trick is not to be surprised when you discover it doesn't bring you all the happiness and answers you thought it would.

—**PRINCE**, AWARD-WINNING MUSICIAN

If you want others to be happy, practice compassion. If you want to be happy, practice compassion.

—**THE DALAI LAMA**, SPIRITUAL AND POLITICAL LEADER

You must try to generate happiness within yourself. If you aren't happy in one place, chances are you won't be happy anyplace.

—**ERNIE BANKS**, FORMER PLAYER FOR THE CHICAGO CUBS

You can find people rich, powerful, and famous, and they aren't happy. And you can find people who have discovered the fact that it's really helping people, it's really being compassionate toward other human beings that makes you happy.

—**GEORGE LUCAS**, DIRECTOR OF *STAR WARS* MOVIES

If you love what you do—whether you're an auto mechanic or you sew clothes or you cook—it's all about personal passion and love that really makes the thrust to the level that you want to get it to.

—**EMERIL LAGASSE**, CHEF AND TV HOST

It is not how much we have, but how much we enjoy that makes happiness.

—**WOODY ALLEN**, SCREENWRITER, ACTOR, AND FILM DIRECTOR

This is what I do, not who I am, and I don't rely on these things for my happiness. I think I have a strong spiritual base because I get up in the morning and say my prayers, thankful to be alive. I keep it simple and I work to remain humble.

—**DENZEL WASHINGTON**, AWARD-WINNING ACTOR

I'm gonna live my life and be the person that I want to be. And do the right thing.

—**TOM CRUISE**, STAR OF THE *MISSION IMPOSSIBLE* MOVIES

The best way to cheer yourself up is to try to cheer somebody else up.

—**MARK TWAIN**, AUTHOR OF *THE ADVENTURES OF HUCKLEBERRY FINN*

WHY DO YOU KEEP GIVING ME WEIRD ADVICE?

PROVERBS ARE SHORT SENTENCES BASED ON LONG EXPERIENCE.

I'VE GOT A PROVERB FOR YOU, TOO. WANNA HEAR IT?

SURE!

FREE ADVICE IS WORTH EXACTLY WHAT YOU PAID FOR IT!

THE 10TH NINJA SECRET TO
BEING A TOTALLY UNSTOPPABLE KID

HOW TO FIGHT
YOUR OWN BATTLES

(SELF-RELIANCE)

Have you ever noticed how other people are always ready to give you advice—even when you haven't asked them for any? Never forget that you are responsible for your own decisions. Looking to other people for advice might give you important insight, but you should never leave your dreams and goals in the hands of others. It's your life, after all!

Here's a neat trick to use when you can't decide whether to follow the crowd or to follow your heart:

Think about your problem, and then write down what your instincts tell you to do about it. After you write down your heart's solution, create two columns—one with a list of the *worst* things that could happen if you follow your own advice, and then another list right next to it of the *best* things that could happen.

Seeing things listed side by side can have a big effect on how you see your problem. What you'll probably realize is that the very worst thing that could happen really isn't that big of a deal after all. Or maybe you'll realize that you have way more to lose than to gain by taking a foolish risk. Either way, putting things down on paper is a great way to compare your options and to solve problems on your own.●

Your future depends on many things, but mostly on you.

— **FRANK TYGER**, JOURNALIST

Deep down you really have to believe in yourself, and I think everyone that performs at a high level in any sport does.

— **CARL EDWARDS**, RACE CAR DRIVER

What's money? A man is a success if he gets up in the morning and gets to bed at night and in between does what he wants to do.

— **BOB DYLAN**, AWARD-WINNING SINGER AND SONGWRITER

Nobody in the rap community thought I could go from music to being successful in a TV show. Their doubt was what I needed. All it takes is just one person telling me I can't do it and I'll use the fear of failure as fuel. I might get knocked out, but I'm going to fail swinging.

— **WILL SMITH**, STAR OF THE MOVIES *HANCOCK* AND *I AM LEGEND*

There are no extraordinary men, just extraordinary circumstances that ordinary men are forced to deal with.

> —**WILLIAM HALSEY**, ADMIRAL

Every tub must stand on its own bottom.

> —**THOMAS FULLER**, MINISTER AND
> PHYSICIAN

The best bet is to bet on yourself.

> —**ARNOLD GLASOW**, PUBLISHER

We skim the top of the clouds and the sun is coming up over the hills and everything is lined in silver. It was so magical, an epiphany. I knew I wanted to be in the sky.

> —**SEAN TUCKER**, STUNT PILOT

The opportunities for enjoyment in life are limitless. If you feel you are not experiencing enough joy, you have only yourself to blame.

> —**DAVID E. BRESLER**, NEUROSCIENTIST AND
> EDUCATOR

I am the master of my fate; I am the captain of my soul.

—**WILLIAM E. HENLEY**, POET

Fair play with others is primarily not blaming them for anything that is wrong with us.

—**ERIC HOFFER**, PHILOSOPHER

Men are made stronger on realization that the helping hand they need is at the end of their own arm.

—**SIDNEY J. PHIL**, POET

Thinking is like loving and dying. Each of us must do it for himself.

—**JOSIAH ROYCE**, PHILOSOPHER

Every man paddles his own canoe.

—**FREDERICK MARRYAT**, NOVELIST

Nothing can bring you peace but yourself.

—**RALPH WALDO EMERSON**, PHILOSOPHER
AND POET

At the age of six I wanted to be a cook. At seven I wanted to be Napoleon. And my ambition has been growing steadily ever since.

—**SALVADOR DALI**, SURREALIST PAINTER

It's empowering, not becoming a prisoner of some other person's idea of what you should be.

—**MATT DAMON**, ACTOR BEST KNOWN FOR WRITING, DIRECTING, AND STARRING IN *GOOD WILL HUNTING*

You are always going to be criticized if you're a doer. You have to make sure you know who to listen to. You need to pick out certain people you have great respect for and listen to them.

—**ROBERT BALLARD**, EXPLORER

It's not how much you have at any given moment, but whether you are improving or not improving. I decided that I'm going to make something out of my life and be happy.

—**JEONG KIM**, ENGINEER AND PRESIDENT OF BELL LABS

That's why I love doing what I do because I can get up one day and feel a little country and throw my cowboy boots on and I'm a cowboy and I feel just like me. The next day, I can throw on my baggies and put my hat backwards and be a little more hip hop, and feel just like me. It all feels very natural to me, that I can be different people all the time.

—**KID ROCK**, AWARD-WINNING MUSICIAN

Skating first appealed to me because of the type of people that did it, plus the fact it wasn't organized or coached. There was no "perfect swing" to master; everybody did things their own way and every way seemed "right."

—**RODNEY MULLEN**, SKATEBOARDER

My interest is in the future because I am going to spend the rest of my life there.

—**CHARLES F. KETTERING**, INVENTOR AND HOLDER OF OVER 300 PATENTS

Somebody's boring me; I think it's me.

—**DYLAN THOMAS**, POET

THE 11TH NINJA SECRET TO BEING A TOTALLY UNSTOPPABLE KID

HOW TO KNOW WHAT REALLY MATTERS

(PUTTING THINGS IN PERSPECTIVE)

So you're not Einstein. You got a C on your math test even though you studied. And that yearly Presidential Fitness Challenge? You couldn't do a single pull-up, no matter how hard you strained and how much you grunted.

On the surface, it blows.

But when you think about it, *really* think about it, how much does a single quiz matter? A failed pull-up may seem important for a moment, especially when half the class watched you drop to the floor, but it's truly a grain of sand compared to the mountain that is your life.

When you stress out about everything, you can't focus on what's really important: spending time with family and friends, finding your unique talents, and enjoying simple things like a sunny day or walk with your dog. Sometimes it helps to make a list—whether it's in your head or you write it down on paper—of those simple things that make you happy.

But shaking off life's bummers doesn't mean forgetting them. You don't have to be the school's best athlete, but you can be physically fit. Walking and riding a bike are fun ways to stay in shape without facing competitive pressure. Working on math is important, but you may discover your true talent lies in art or computers or writing. The point is to focus on what's really important to you.

It doesn't matter what you call the good stuff in your life—blessings, gifts, or just good luck. All that matters is that you think about that good stuff each and every day.●

When we create our dreams, there's always going
to be some part of the creation that isn't what we
prefer. That's part of the game. We're always going to
have challenges, self-doubt, uncertainty, screw ups,
pain, and pleasure. Truthfully, if we ever got there in
every area, we'd be bored stiff.

—**JAMES ARTHUR RAY**, WRITER AND
THOUGHT LEADER

Friends are the sunshine of life.

—**JOHN HAY**, DIPLOMAT AND WRITER

I've been poor with millions of dollars, and I've been
rich when I was broke. Money never gave me any
real joy, but with God in my heart I'm a rich man no
matter what.

—**GEORGE FOREMAN**, BOXER AND OLYMPIC
GOLD MEDALIST

Simplicity, clarity, and singleness: These are the attri-
butes that give our lives power and vividness and joy.

—**RICHARD HALLOWAY**, WRITER AND
BROADCASTER

Religion, if it's real, can't be a sometime thing. It can't be a Sunday thing.

> —**MARTIN SHEEN**, ACTOR WHO PLAYED THE PRESIDENT IN *THE WEST WING*

May you live all the days of your life.

> —**JONATHAN SWIFT**, SATIRIST

Love and time—those are the only two things in all the world and all of life that cannot be bought, but only spent.

> —**GARY JENNINGS**, WRITER

There is only one meaning of life, the act of living itself.

> —**ERICH FROMM**, PHILOSOPHER AND PSYCHOLOGIST

For the vast majority of children's authors, it is not a lucrative career. If you are looking to make lots of money, I recommend getting into crime.

> —**MO WILLEMS**, WRITER AND ILLUSTRATOR

I wish I could stand on a busy corner, hat in hand, and beg people to throw me all their wasted hours.

—**BERNARD BERENSON**, ART HISTORIAN

It isn't hard to be good from time to time in sports. What's tough is being good every day.

—**WILLIE MAYS**, ACCLAIMED BASEBALL PLAYER

I get a lot of my spirituality through nature, which gives me a lot of inspiration in capturing beauty. Beauty is sort of like nature's way of having you fall in love with something. If you fall in love with something, then you'll protect it.

—**LOUIS SCHWARTZBERG**, DOCUMENTARY FILMMAKER

The success is great. But we wrote our last record while we were being dropped and playing for 10 people. We know what it's like to do it just for fun.

—**NICK JONAS**, MUSICIAN AND MEMBER OF THE JONAS BROTHERS

There is no greatness where there is not simplicity.

> —**LEO TOLSTOY**, WRITER BEST KNOWN FOR NOVELS *ANNA KARENINA* AND *WAR AND PEACE*

My formula for living is quite simple. I get up in the morning and I go to bed at night. In between I occupy myself as best I can.

> —**CARY GRANT**, FILM ACTOR

I started [snowboarding] way back in the day when it was friends and family making snowboards—nobody was cut-throating here and there. Now it's politics and dollar signs, but I guess that's the business.

> —**MATT GOODWILL**, SNOWBOARDER

I just returned from a fund raiser and fashion show, with live commentating, and at the end, 600 people were applauding, which was wonderful, but the best thing was to arrive home on Sunday morning and have my kids all jump up to give me a hug. Hugs from my kids are the best. They make it all worth it.

> —**ALEXANDER JULIAN**, FASHION DESIGNER

As you get older, you realize you need balance. If it's not fun, what's the point?

—**BEN STILLER**, AWARD-WINNING ACTOR
AND STAR OF *ZOOLANDER*

Peace of mind is worth more than a million bucks to me.

—**STEVE ALBINI**, RECORD PRODUCER

Take your profession seriously; don't take yourself seriously.

—**CLINT EASTWOOD**, AWARD-WINNING
ACTOR, DIRECTOR, AND ANTI-HERO

You know how cruel kids can be. I was mocked and taunted, but the experience made me stronger.

—**GEORGE CLOONEY**, AWARD-WINNING
ACTOR KNOWN FOR *ER* AND *OCEAN'S
ELEVEN*

Just to be is a blessing. Just to live is holy.

—**ABRAHAM HESCHEL**, RABBI

THE 12TH NINJA SECRET TO BEING A TOTALLY UNSTOPPABLE KID

HOW TO BE A MAN OF ACTION

(TURNING WORDS INTO ACTIONS)

What's the difference between a kid who *wants* a role in the school play and the kid who *has* a role in the school play? Not just talent. The kid who won the role practiced his audition and then tried out for the play. He didn't just dream about it—he did it!

You're in charge of your wish list. Want a new friend? Then you've got to find the courage and ask that person to hang out with you. Want a new video game? Then you've got to mow a neighbor's lawn or do something to earn the cash. The distance between what you've got and what you want is measured by action.

Some boys sit around hoping a genie will pop out of a bottle and offer them three wishes. (But you're so smart, you'd wish for more wishes, right?!) They grumble and whine, but they never do anything to turn their wishes into reality. The do-nothing strategy is not only annoying; it's a guaranteed dream-killer.

Consider two ideas to help get what you want:

Ask others about how they got what they wanted. Learn from the steps they took—and from their mistakes.

Write down what you want. Then break your goal down into smaller, simple tasks that lead up to the bigger goal.

If you asked a billionaire how he made it, he might admit that he got some lucky breaks along the way. But his road to success probably was made of miles and miles of action. ●

If you aren't going all the way, why go at all?

—**JOE NAMATH**, FOOTBALL PLAYER ELECTED
TO THE HALL OF FAME

Don't let the noise of others' opinions drown out
your own inner voice.

—**STEVE JOBS**, COFOUNDER AND CEO OF
APPLE

My parents never tried to influence my decisions.
They pretty much left it up to me. I wasn't a troubled
child. I was doing well in school, so they said to do
what you like, which is the same attitude I now have
with my own kids: "Just do what you like. You have
to pursue what you're interested in. Just do it well,
whatever you pick."

—**DAVID HO**, AIDS RESEARCHER

Do it big or stay in bed.

—**LARRY KELLEY**, FOOTBALL PLAYER

The future is one I must make myself.

—**LOUIS L'AMOUR**, WRITER

Procrastination is one of the most common and deadliest of diseases and its toll on success and happiness is heavy.

—**WAYNE GRETZKY**, HOCKEY PLAYER AND MEMBER OF THE HOCKEY HALL OF FAME

But it's not athletic ability that really counts. It's that inner quality of persistence and belief that makes the difference, that totally awesome commitment to change.

—**BOB HARPER**, CELEBRITY TRAINER

Part of what makes us go, part of our heart as a band, has to do with running things ourselves. Had we given up that part, it would have destroyed us.

—**IAN MACKAYE**, MUSICIAN AND MEMBER OF FUGAZI

What counts is not necessarily the size of the dog in the fight, but the size of the fight in the dog.

—**DWIGHT EISENHOWER**, 34TH PRESIDENT OF THE UNITED STATES

The only failure I know is never making the attempt.

—**GEORGE CLOONEY**, AWARD-WINNING ACTOR KNOWN FOR ER AND OCEAN'S ELEVEN

Just because a man lacks the use of his eyes doesn't mean he lacks vision.

—**STEVIE WONDER**, AWARD-WINNING BLIND SINGER AND SONGWRITER

I wrote a record like that called "Heartbreaker." Everyone loves that record, but when I hear that I want to punch myself in the mouth, because I sound like I'm blaming everyone for my problems. It's more important to write songs where you can get some kind of perspective and be honest. If you feel victimized romantically, like I have, the best thing is to try and find out where the other person is coming from.

—**RYAN ADAMS**, MUSICIAN

Not being able to govern others, I govern myself.

—**MICHEL DE MONTAIGNE**, WRITER AND ESSAYIST

When someone slams your writing, listen carefully to what they say. Then tell yourself that he or she is a tasteless, moronic, jealous, mean-spirited, ignorant jerk. Then go back to your garret and figure out what you did wrong.

—**PETE HAUTMAN**, WRITER

I did something then, almost 40 years ago, only 22 years old, that I still do now. I decided I had nothing to lose, so I was just myself.

—**LARRY KING**, BROADCASTER

No hope, no action.

—**PETER LEVI**, ARCHAEOLOGIST AND WRITER

One's self image is very important because if that's in good shape, then you can do anything, or practically anything.

—**SIR JOHN GIELGUD**, BRITISH ACTOR AND SINGER

Great poetry is always written by somebody straining to go beyond what he can do.

—STEPHEN SPENDER, POET LAUREATE

Skill and confidence are an unconquered army.

—GEORGE HERBERT, POET AND PRIEST

Heaven and hell is right now.... You make it heaven or you make it hell by your actions.

—GEORGE HARRISON, FORMER LEAD GUITARIST IN THE BEATLES

I am, indeed, a king, because I know how to rule myself.

—PIETRO ARETINO, WRITER

I count him braver who overcomes his desires than him who conquers his enemies; the hardest victory is the victory over self.

—ARISTOTLE, GREEK PHILOSOPHER

THE 13TH NINJA SECRET TO BEING A TOTALLY UNSTOPPABLE KID

HOW TO READ YOUR INNER COMPASS

(DOING THE RIGHT THING)

You never claimed to be a saint. Never wanted a ton of merit badges. Never asked to win the Boy of the Year award in some national honesty contest. But sooner or later you will have to choose between right and wrong—whether to look away or take a stand.

Maybe you'll be at the gas station, buying a soft drink with a buddy. And while you're walking to the cashier, you see your pal slip a candy bar in his pocket. Or maybe at school, you'll hear a classmate brag about copying her research report from the Internet. Whatever the situation, you're in a rotten place. Do you rat out a friend?

Look the other way? Let him get away with shoplifting, but later, tell him only losers steal?

You have to look into your own heart for the answer. You have to decide what *you* think is right and then live it each and every day. That might mean giving up a friendship because your friend doesn't share your values. That might mean telling an adult. It might mean some of your buddies think you're lame because you ratted them out.

But what really matters is what you think. Kids and adults need to be able to fall asleep each night knowing they've done the right thing. Having true peace in your heart is more important than having a moment of false peace at that gas station while your buddy leaves the store without paying.

Your friends will come around. They know what's right and wrong, too. Some people just need more time to get to the answer. ●

You do not become good by trying to be good, but by finding the goodness that is already within you, and allowing that goodness to emerge.

—ECKHART TOLLE, SPIRITUAL TEACHER AND WRITER

Men expect too much, do too little.

—ALLEN TATE, POET

Consciousness is the people, men and women, who immediately go to where there's an earthquake and, without recognition, they heal, feed, or bury. Or, very quietly, just their presence elevates others. It's the most important thing you can do on this planet, to elevate, transform, and illumine your own consciousness.

—CARLOS SANTANA, ACCLAIMED GUITARIST

I realized that I had no power to correct a situation and only a greater force did. And that put my life into perspective. I'm just passing through and all I want to do is leave behind some good footprints.

—SYLVESTER STALLONE, STAR OF *ROCKY*

The time is always right to do what is right.

> —**MARTIN LUTHER KING JR.**, CIVIL RIGHTS
> LEADER

Life is the sum of all your choices.

> —**ALBERT CAMUS**, PHILOSOPHER AND
> WRITER

Wherever you see a successful business, someone
once made a courageous decision.

> —**PETER DRUCKER**, WRITER AND
> MANAGEMENT CONSULTANT

If you think too long, you think wrong.

> —**JIM KAAT**, BASEBALL PLAYER AND
> SPORTSCASTER

Not to decide is to decide.

> —**HARVEY COX**, THEOLOGIAN

Pick battles big enough to matter, small enough
to win.

    —**JONATHAN KOZOL**, WRITER AND ACTIVIST

Trust your own instinct. Your mistakes might as well
be your own instead of someone else's.

    —**BILLY WILDER**, WRITER, DIRECTOR, AND
      PRODUCER

I think character is what you're doing when nobody
else is around.

    —**PEYTON MANNING**, FOOTBALL PLAYER AND
      THREE-TIME NFL MVP

Learn from the past if you want what matters in
the present.

    —**MASSIMO VIGNELLI**, DESIGNER

How far would Moses have gone if he had taken a
poll in Egypt?

    —**HARRY S. TRUMAN**, 33RD PRESIDENT OF
      THE UNITED STATES

In case of doubt, decide in favor of what is correct.

— **KARL KRAUS**, WRITER

Where people of goodwill get together and transcend their differences for the common good, peaceful and just solutions can be found, even for those problems that seem most intractable.

— **NELSON MANDELA**, CIVIL RIGHTS LEADER
AND FIRST BLACK MAN TO BE PRESIDENT
OF SOUTH AFRICA

My mother was a person who would never accept an excuse from my brother or myself. If you came with an excuse, she would always say, "Do you have a brain?" And if the answer was yes, then you had a way to get around it. Maybe you should use the brain.

— **BENJAMIN CARSON**, PEDIATRIC
NEUROSURGEON

It's easy to have principles when you're rich. The important thing is to have principles when you're poor.

— **RAY KROC**, MCDONALD'S FOUNDER

A person's character is what it is. It's a little like a marriage—only without the option of divorce. You can work on it and try to make it better, but basically you have to take the bitter with the sweet.

—HENDRICK HERTZBERG, JOURNALIST

If you start a business because you think you're going to make a lot of money at it, then you probably won't be successful because that's the wrong reason to start a business. You have to really believe in what you're doing

—PIERRE OMIDYAR, EBAY FOUNDER

This may sound funny, but I'm not a risk taker. I consider myself a risk manager, and I take safety really, really seriously. I follow a philosophy that I call the "P factor": Proper planning and preparation prevent a piss-poor performance.

—LEWIS GORDON PUGH, EXTREME SWIMMER

HOW TO SEE
THROUGH BRICK WALLS
(CHANGING THE WAY YOU LOOK AT THINGS)

Fact: You wear your big brother's old clothes.

Fact: You don't have the latest iPod or your own smartphone.

Fact: Your parents drive an old, ugly minivan with a big dent over the bumper.

Conclusion: You're not cool because you don't have any money.

Wrong! It's easy to look at your life like it's some kind of brick wall that you can't get over, through, or around. But if you change how you think, you'll change the way you see your life. Thoughts become reality. The way we think shapes the way we feel, what we believe, and how we act.

If you think about the stuff you own as precious gifts, you'll soon see your brother's cotton hoodie as your most comfortable shirt and the rusty minivan as the way to fun times at school games, friends' parties, and the mall. A C on a math test is major bummer if you think grades are more important than learning. On the other hand, if you've studied hard, paid attention in class, and focused on learning, a C is a grade worth celebrating.

People sense your thought and beliefs, and they'll adopt them. If you think you're a loser because your family doesn't have money, then your classmates will begin to see you that way, too. That's because your reputation isn't built on money or a lack of money. Your reputation, and the way you see yourself, is built on your thoughts, feelings, and actions. Change those and that imaginary brick wall disappears, allowing you to go wherever you like and become whoever you want to be.●

I can honestly say that there is no point in becoming obsessed by what could have, should have or might have been.

—**CHRISTOPHER REEVES**, ACTOR, ACTIVIST, AND STAR OF *SUPERMAN*

Don't let criticism get in the way of learning. Whatever negative comments a teacher or a college professor or even your family may make, consider them. Take it as an opportunity to see your work with a different perspective.

—**DANA LEVIN**, PAINTER

I had a simpler perspective on life when I was younger. At that time, my goals were more about winning and success. Now that I'm older, I know there's more to life than that.

—**TAKEHIKO INOUE**, MANGA ARTIST

Education should be the process of helping everyone to discover his uniqueness.

—**LEO BUSCAGLIA**, WRITER, PROFESSOR, AND MOTIVATIONAL SPEAKER

What's a joy to the one is a nightmare to the other.
  —BERTOLT BRECHT, WRITER

What's important is finding out what works for you.
  —HENRY MOORE, SCULPTOR

I'd rather be a failure at something I enjoy than a success as something I hate.
  —GEORGE BURNS, COMEDIAN

I'm a salami writer. I try to write good salami, but salami is salami.
  —STEPHEN KING, WRITER

Be what you are. This is the first step toward becoming better than you are.
  —JULIUS CHARLES HARE, THEOLOGIAN

You gotta be a man to play baseball for a living, but you gotta have a lot of little boy in you, too.
  —ROY CAMPANELLA, BASEBALL PLAYER

We are betrayed by what is false within.

—**GEORGE MEREDITH**, WRITER AND POET

If a man is called to be a street sweeper, he should sweep streets even as Michelangelo painted, or Beethoven composed music, or Shakespeare wrote poetry. He should sweep streets so well that all the hosts of heaven and earth will pause to say, here lived a great street sweeper who did his job well.

—**MARTIN LUTHER KING, JR.**, CIVIL RIGHTS LEADER

Big changes in our lives are more or less a second chance.

—**HARRISON FORD**, STAR OF THE *INDIANA JONES* MOVIES

Unless you're ready to think, feel, and act in different ways than you've done prior to now, you'll continue to live the life that you're living with the results you've been getting.

—**JAMES ARTHUR RAY**, WRITER AND THOUGHT LEADER

It is better to be hated for what you are than loved for what you are not.

> —**ANDRE GIDE**, NOBEL PRIZE WINNER FOR LITERATURE

We are sure to be losers when we quarrel with ourselves: it is civil war.

> —**CHARLES CALEB COLTON**, WRITER AND CLERIC

Nobody is so miserable as he who longs to be somebody other than the person he is.

> —**ANGELO PATRI**, WRITER AND EDUCATOR

As you make each passage from youth to adulthood to maturity, sometimes you put your arms up and scream, sometimes you just hang on to that bar in front of you. But the ride is the thing. I think the most you can hope for at the end of life is that your hair's messed, you're out of breath, and you didn't throw up.

> —**JERRY SEINFELD**, COMEDIAN, ACTOR, AND STAR OF *SEINFELD*

If a man has a talent and cannot use it, he has failed. If he has a talent and uses half of it, he has partly failed. If he has a talent and learns somehow to use the whole of it, he has gloriously succeeded and won a satisfaction and a triumph few men ever know.

—THOMAS WOLFE, WRITER

Young people who pretend to be wise to the ways of the world are mostly just cynics. Cynicism masquerades as wisdom, but it is the farthest thing from it. Because cynics don't learn anything. Because cynicism is a self-imposed blindness, a rejection of the world because we are afraid it will hurt us or disappoint us.

—STEPHEN COLBERT, COMEDIAN

It doesn't matter what your own worst moment is. Storms of all kinds rage through our lives, and sometimes they can take everything from us. But if you have faith, your own worst moment can become your best.

—GEORGE FOREMAN, BOXER AND OLYMPIC
    GOLD MEDALIST

THE 15TH NINJA SECRET TO BEING A TOTALLY UNSTOPPABLE KID

WHEN TO DOUBLE DOG DARE YOURSELF

(TAKING RISKS)

Anyone can nail easy skateboarding tricks. But the first time you pull off a 50-50 grind, you know why it's cool to take a risk. You feel like you can conquer the world!

Risks are more than daredevil stunts, though. Risks are about doing anything new or different, and every kid has his own idea of what's risky. Consider this: Trying out for band is a risk when you're the school's best basketball player. Saying hi to the coolest girl in school is risk when you're the quiet kid in the back row. If the thought of doing something new makes your heart race and your stomach churn, it's probably a risk!

When you try something new, sometimes you blow it. The star basketball player worries his first saxophone solo will sound like burping geese instead of smooth jazz. Everyone stresses out when they venture into new territory.

Boys who dare to be different and try new things are fun to be around. They're the ones who introduce everyone else to a new website, taco joint, or video game. They're interesting because they always have something new to share.

Without risks, life would be one big yawn. Imagine if you were still hanging out with the exact same people and doing the exact same things as you did in first grade. You'd have a life free of stress and failure but full of boredom.

Taking a risk means you're taking on the chance of failing, but most of the time your risk turns into a success. That saxophone solo is flawless, and the coolest girl in school smiles and says hi back. ●

I like it when things are pushed just a little too far.

—**STEVE CARELL**, ACTOR IN *LITTLE MISS SUNSHINE* AND *GET SMART*

I'd rather see different people in the crowd every time we play a show than see the same people, the same fashions, the same social strata. It's way more exciting to play to different kinds of people than it is to play to the same people over and over again.

—**BEN GIBBARD**, MUSICIAN AND LEAD SINGER OF DEATH CAB FOR CUTIE

Follow your bliss. Find where it is and don't be afraid to follow it.

—**JOSEPH CAMPBELL**, WRITER AND MYTHOLOGIST

Ignorance is bliss. Knowing what a hard business restaurants are and the failure rate, I don't think I would be as good at starting it now. I think it helps to be bold and unafraid.

—**STEVE ELLS**, FOUNDER OF CHIPOTLE

Any life truly lived is a risky business, and if one puts up too many fences against the risks one ends by shutting out life itself.

—**KENNETH S. DAVIS**, HISTORIAN

If you don't take chances, you can't do anything in life.

—**MICHAEL SPINKS**, BOXER AND OLMPIC
GOLD MEDAL WINNER

There's no such thing as a sure thing. That's why they call it gambling.

—**NEIL SIMON**, WRITER

The fishermen know that the sea is dangerous and the storm terrible, but they have never found these dangers sufficient reason for remaining ashore.

—**VINCENT VAN GOGH**, EXPRESSIONIST
PAINTER

For every role that I have done on TV and movies, I've auditioned for 30 or 40.

—**ZAC EFRON**, ACTOR AND SIBGER

The bungee jumping and the skydiving only serve as metaphors for choices that (people) make in other areas of their lives. So when they leap off that bridge, they are leaping into the unknown, and having done something like that they are then more likely to leap in other unexplored areas of life.

> —**PHIL KEOGHAN**, AWARD-WINNING TELEVISION HOST

Be bold and mighty forces will come to your aid.

> —**BASIL KING**, WRITER AND MINISTER

Taking risks gives me energy.

> —**JAY CHIAT**, DESIGNER

No one would have crossed the ocean if he could have gotten off the ship in the storm.

> —**CHARLES KETTERING**, INVENTOR AND HOLDER OF OVER 300 PATENTS

In order to find the edge, you must risk going over the edge.

> —**DENNIS DUGAN**, ACTOR AND DIRECTOR

If you limit your actions in life to things that nobody can possibly find fault with, you will not do much.

　　—**LEWIS CARROLL**, AUTHOR OF *ALICE'S ADVENTURES IN WONDERLAND*

I don't like everything we do. At the time, you mean it to be the best, but I'm still critical of every record Cheap Trick has made, and I hope I continue that way.

　　—**RICK NIELSEN**, MUSICIAN IN CHEAP TRICK

Now will saying "yes" get you in trouble at times? Will saying "yes" lead you to doing some foolish things? Yes, it will. But don't be afraid to be a fool. Remember, you cannot be both young and wise.

　　—**STEPHEN COLBERT**, COMEDIAN

To play it safe is not to play.

　　—**ROBERT ALTMAN**, FILM DIRECTOR

Dare to be naïve.

　　—**R. BUCKMINSTER FULLER**, DESIGNER AND INVENTOR

It's not natural to go onstage in front of 3,000 people and perform. You have to love it and want to do it, and it scares the hell out of me every night, but it's a good kind of scared.

—**MARK MCGRATH**, MUSICIAN AND SINGER
IN SUGAR RAY

The trap for an actor is that you become too successful at what you're trying to do, and you can find yourself stuck there. As an actor, there's so many ways that it can go wrong for you, and so few ways it can go right.

—**BEN AFFLECK**, AWARD-WINNING ACTOR
AND CO-STAR IN *GOOD WILL HUNTING*

Perhaps this is the rationale of all risky sports. You deliberately raise the ante of effort and concentration in order, as it were, to clear your mind of trivialities. It's a small-scale model for living, but with a difference: Unlike your routine life, where mistakes can usually be recouped and some kind of compromise patched up, your actions, for however brief a period, are deadly serious.

—**A. ALVAREZ**, WRITER

129

WEREN'T YOU GOING TO THE BATTING CAGES?

I *WAS*...

...BUT I CAN'T FIND MY BAT.

WE'RE GOING TO A GAME AT THE STADIUM.

WANNA COME ALONG?

SURE...

BEATS PLAYING BALL BY *MYSELF!*

THE 16TH NINJA SECRET TO
BEING A TOTALLY UNSTOPPABLE KID

HOW TO FOCUS
LIKE A LASER

(KEEPING DREAMS IN SIGHT)

Baseball wouldn't be any fun if you hit homerun after homerun. Okay, not exactly true. Endless homeruns would totally rock for awhile, but pretty soon you'd get bored: Pitch, hit, score. Pitch, hit, score. Strikes and foul balls make the game interesting and motivate you to win.

That's the deal with life, too. All the bumps along the way make your goals and dreams even more enticing. And when you finally achieve those goals, they're that much more satisfying. Think of how amazing your favorite pizza tastes when you're really hungry.

The baseball rule applies to everything:

Your parents won't let you go to a party because your grandparents are visiting. That's a strike. But your grandparents are happy because they love spending time with you and, as much as you hate to admit it, they can be pretty cool. And the next time you have fun with your friends, you really appreciate the good time.

You want the lead role in the class play but you get chosen to be the lead character's crazy sidekick. That's a strike. But it turns out the crazy sidekick gets the best lines and steals the show. Maybe you prove yourself and land the lead in the next show.

You want to be an astronaut, but your grade in math is proof you'll never master physics. That's a strike. But if you keep asking your teacher for help, maybe even get a tutor, you can boost your knowledge and grades.

If you stay positive and learn to refocus when things don't go as you've planned, you'll turn your dreams into reality. ●

I can't live without music. I don't think I physically could live without music because it's the thing that allows me to feel normal.

—**BONO**, LEAD SINGER OF U2

I cannot live or think without painting. I think that I became an artist when I first took the brushes, mixed the paints, put them on canvas, and my soul appeared in the painting.

—**NICK JAPARIDZE**, PAINTER

And the only way to do great work is to love what you do. If you haven't found it yet, keep looking. Don't settle. As with all matters of the heart, you'll know when you find it.

—**STEVE JOBS**, COFOUNDER AND CEO OF APPLE

I really, really love what I'm doing. People survive longer if they love what they're doing. Because you just don't quit.

—**KENNY ROGERS**, COUNTRY MUSIC SINGER AND SONGWRITER

Music has always been central to my life, much more so than acting. Acting is how I make my living. Music has always been a passion—it's something I love, something I can't live without.

    —JOHN CORBETT, ACTOR AND COUNTRY MUSIC SINGER

When you get your first laugh, like at six years old, and I pretend to fall down, and people laugh. And just something tingles in your brain. And you're like, "Oh, I want more of this." And if there's any way to get paid doing it, wow. Utopia.

    —MATTHEW PERRY, ACTOR KNOWN FOR STARRING IN *FRIENDS*

Writing is not enough for me. I did not come here to just be a writer. I live to play. I'm not here to take a stab at it. I am going to DO it.

    —JAMEY JOHNSON, COUNTRY MUSICIAN

The soul that has no established aim loses itself.

    —MICHEL DE MONTAIGNE, WRITER AND ESSAYIST

Destiny is not a matter of chance, it is a matter of choice; it is not a thing to be waited for, it is a thing to be achieved.

—**WILLIAM JENNINGS BRYAN**, POLITICIAN
AND LAWYER

Not failure, but low aim, is crime.

—**JAMES RUSSELL LOWELL**, POET AND
DIPLOMAT

Happiness is essentially a state of going somewhere, wholeheartedly, one-directionally, without regret or reservation.

—**WILLIAM H. SHELDON**, PSYCHOLOGIST

The poor man is not he who is without a cent, but he who is without a dream.

—**HARRY KEMP**, POET

There is one thing which gives radiance to everything. It is the idea of something around the corner.

—**G. K. CHESTERTON**, WRITER

Dream as if you'll live forever. Live as if you'll die today.

> —**JAMES DEAN**, ACTOR AND STAR OF *REBEL WITHOUT A CAUSE*

I just make records because I want people to come see my show. Recording music for folks to just listen to music is great, but I've got to be out there on stage making it.

> —**MARK CHESNUTT**, COUNTRY MUSIC SINGER

The purpose of life is a life of purpose.

> —**ROBERT BYRNE**, CHESS PLAYER

Follow your bliss. Find where it is and don't be afraid to follow it.

> —**JOSEPH CAMPBELL**, WRITER AND MYTHOLOGIST

Nobody ever remembers who finished second at anything.

> —**JACK NICKLAUS**, GOLFER AND MEMBER OF THE WORLD GOLF HALL OF FAME

Great minds have purposes, others have wishes.

> —**WASHINGTON IRVING**, WRITER AND
> HISTORIAN

The tragedy in life doesn't lie in not reaching your goal. The tragedy lies in having no goal to reach.

> —**BENJAMIN MAYS**, MINISTER, EDUCATOR
> AND ACTIVIST

You have to have a dream so you can get up in the morning.

> —**BILLY WILDER**, WRITER, DIRECTOR, AND
> PRODUCER

Be a life long or short. Its completeness depends on what it was lived for.

> —**DAVID STARR** JORDAN, EDUCATOR AND
> ACTIVIST

He turns not back who is bound to a star.

> —**LEONARDO DA VINCI**, PAINTER BEST
> KNOWN FOR *MONA LISA* AND *THE LAST
> SUPPER*

THE 17TH NINJA SECRET TO
BEING A TOTALLY UNSTOPPABLE KID

HOW TO SEE WHAT
OTHERS CAN'T

(TRUSTING YOURSELF)

There's a new guy in school and he seems funny
and cool. When you mention he might be fun
to hang around, your friends sneer like you just
offered them cockroach pizza. What's with *that*?
Does he drool in his food or slaughter puppies
or something?

This is one of those times where you should
trust your gut. Ask him to hang out and test
your first reaction. He cracked you up in gym
class, but do you really share a sense of humor?
Do you really like to do the same things?

He might become one of your best friends,
and chances are your buddies will warm up to

him, too. And if you don't like him, that's okay, because you discovered it yourself. You didn't let someone else tell you what to think.

Sometimes people in your life think they know you better than you know yourself. It's not just friends—it's parents, older siblings, and grand-parents. They've known you since birth, so they definitely know you well. But that doesn't mean they have the blueprints to your brain and heart.

It's never good to shut out the words of people who love you, but growing up means learning to rely on your own judgment. You probably told your parents about all your problems when you were little—from having had a cranky teacher to the bully who terrorized everyone at the bus stop. But now, you're probably thinking more things through and finding your own answers.

When you do what your heart tells you, you gain confidence in your decisions. You learn that first and foremost, you can trust yourself. ●

I don't like to sound egotistical, but every time I stepped up to the plate with a bat in my hands, I couldn't help but feel sorry for the pitcher.

> —**ROGERS HORNSBY**, BASEBALL PLAYER AND TWO-TIME NL MVP

I can't really put a style of mine into words whether they talkin' about rappin' or fashion or production. I just do me.

> —**TUPAC SHAKUR**, RAPPER

How you react to people and situations, especially when challenges arise, is the best indicator of how deeply you know yourself.

> —**ECKHART TOLLE**, SPIRITUAL TEACHER AND WRITER

I always knew even before a race that if I got into a dicey position, I would turn around and race another day rather than take a chance. You just have to figure out how important it is to you.

> —**JOE RUNYAN**, IDITAROD COMPETITOR

If people ask me a question, I want to say what I think, not what I think people want to hear. If I say something I don't believe, then I'm not being myself.

    —SERGIO GARCIA, GOLFER

You can succeed if nobody else believes it, but you will never succeed if you don't believe in yourself.

    —WILLIAM J. H. BOETCKER, MINISTER

As soon as you trust yourself, you will know how to live.

    —JOHANN VON GOETHE, GERMAN WRITER

It is not the yes of others that I am wary of, but my own.

    —NOEL COWARD, PLAYWRIGHT AND ACTOR

Instinct is untaught ability.

    —ALEXANDER BAIN, PHILOSOPHER

The struggle to learn to listen to and respect our own intuitive inner promptings is the greatest challenge of all.

> —**HERB GOLDBERG**, WRITER

Common sense is instinct. Enough of it is genius.

> —**GEORGE BERNARD SHAW**, PLAYWRIGHT

The greatest mistake you can make is to be continually fearing you will make one.

> —**ELBERT HUBBARD**, WRITER AND ARTIST

There are no rules. Just follow your heart.

> —**ROBIN WILLIAMS**, AWARD-WINNING
> ACTOR AND COMEDIAN

I could lie and pretend that I hunt and camp, but that wouldn't be me. Clothes? Shopping? That's stuff I like!

> —**RYAN SEACREST**, TV HOST

Do you know what you are? You are what you is. You are what you am. A cow don't make ham.

—**FRANK ZAPPA**, MUSICIAN

If you do not express your own original ideas, if you do not listen to your own being, you will have betrayed yourself.

—**ROLLO MAY**, PSYCHOLOGIST

I can't take inspiration from books. I've had to learn directly from the world itself. I observe, ask questions, then really listen to the answers.

—**PAUL ORFALEA**, BUSINESS LEADER AND SPEAKER

One of the reasons why so few of us ever act, instead of react, is because we are continually stifling our deepest impulses.

—**HENRY MILLER**, WRITER

Statistics are no substitute for judgment.

—**HENRY CLAY**, STATESMAN AND ORATOR

My fear is that as soon as I get married and have kids, that I'll kind of do what a lot of people do and suddenly start saying, "Now I'm gonna make films for kids." I really hope I don't do that.

—**TREY PARKER**, CO-CREATOR OF *SOUTH PARK*

I have no control over people's perceptions of me at all, and that's one of the things I decided very early on is that I can't control the way other people think of me. All I can do, especially when it comes to my career, is go out there and do cool, unique kinds of things.

—**MACAULAY CULKIN**, ACTOR AND STAR OF *HOME ALONE*

It may not always be easy or pretty, but I'm content trying to be myself as much as possible.

—**MO WILLEMS**, WRITER AND ILLUSTRATOR

If I endorse something or say I'm doing something, then it's getting done and it's getting done right.

—**SOULJA BOY**, RAPPER

THE 18TH NINJA SECRET TO
BEING A TOTALLY UNSTOPPABLE KID

HOW TO GET ALONG
WITH MERE MORTALS
(RESPECTING DIFFERENCES)

Your teacher assigns the class into work groups, and you're stuck with your two least favorite people: the brainiac with frizzy hair and the weirdo who's always banished to the office for makes farting noises with his armpit.

Not exactly your lucky day, but it's one of life's daily tests: How do you act around others, especially the school weirdo, or worse, the single most annoying person in the galaxy? The way you treat people says very little about them— but it says a lot about you.

It's tempting to dislike people who are different because, well, they're different. Strange. Odd.

Even weird. You know everyone has feelings and all that do-unto-others stuff you learned at home or your place of worship. But there seems to be this unspoken school rule: As long as all the other kids are picking on the class weirdo, they're not picking on *me*.

Sometimes breaking through that unspoken rule takes a triple dose of courage. It's easier, though, if you've already made a point of being a respectful person, and if you believe that every single person—no matter how strange they may seem—adds something to our world. Think about living in a place where everyone has the same sense of humor, likes the same things, and excels at the same activities. Sounds as exciting as a knitting tournament, doesn't it?

Here's the other thing about respect. When you give it, you get it. Call it boomerang behavior. When you consistently show people you're a respectful person, respect will fly right back at you!●

Isn't it cheaper and smarter to make friends out of potential enemies than to defend yourself against them later?

—**BONO**, LEAD SINGER OF U2

Deep down, we're all beautiful, but we all have our qualities that we're insecure about. We're all beauties, and we're all geeks.

—**ASHTON KUTCHER**, ACTOR AND PRODUCER

Diversity: the art of thinking independently together.

—**MALCOLM FORBES**, BUSINESSMAN AND PUBLISHER OF *FORBES* MAGAZINE

We teach people how to treat us.

—**DR. PHIL MCGRAW**, TALK SHOW HOST

I don't want to get on a soapbox preaching tolerance, but anything that helps people treat each other with a little more kindness is great.

—**PETER DINKLAGE**, ACTOR

Men are destroyed for being rebellious, and women destroy themselves by failing to be rebellious. Unless you can make that next jump to either getting along with people or resisting people, you are ultimately destroying yourself.

—**CHUCK PALAHNIUK**, NOVELIST BEST KNOWN FOR *FIGHT CLUB*

The most popular persons are those who take the world as it is, who find the least fault.

—**CHARLES DUDLEY WARNER**, WRITER

Before you start to think you should go solve the contradictions and the behavior of others, or other countries or whatever, you should solve the contradictions in yourself.

—**VIGGO MORTENSEN**, ACTOR WHO PLAYED ARAGON IN *THE LORD OF THE RINGS*

A mountain man tries to live with the country instead of against it.

—**LOUIS L'AMOUR**, WRITER

Bitterness imprisons life; love releases it.

   —**HARRY EMERSON FOSDICK**, MINISTER

To forgive is the highest, most beautiful form of love. In return, you will receive untold peace and happiness.

   —**ROBERT MULLER**, DIPLOMAT

We are so cold to others only when we are dull in ourselves.

   —**WILLIAM HAZLITT**, WRITER

Happiness . . . is achieved only by making others happy.

   —**STUART CLOETE**, WRITER

Goodness is the only investment that never fails.

   —**HENRY DAVID THOREAU**, PHILOSOPHER

No man is more cheated than the selfish man.

   —**HENRY WARD BEECHER**, ACTIVIST

Acceptance is the truest kinship with humanity.

—G. K. CHESTERTON, WRITER

To carry a grudge is like being stung to death by one bee.

—WILLIAM H. WALTON, COMPOSER

Hate is a prolonged form of suicide.

—DOUGLAS V. STEERE, THEOLOGIAN AND PHILOSOPHER

I believe that pride in yourself is very important. I think pride in your race is very important. But then there's got to be something more, and that is tolerance.

—SIMON BAKER, STAR OF *THE MENTALIST*

Probably no greater honor can come to any man than the respect of his colleagues.

—CARY GRANT, FILM ACTOR

I learned that to humiliate another person is to make him suffer an unnecessarily cruel fate.

>—**NELSON MANDELA**, CIVIL RIGHTS LEADER
>   AND FIRST BLACK MAN TO BE PRESIDENT
>   OF SOUTH AFRICA

Living well and beautifully and justly are all one thing.

>—**SOCRATES**, PHILOSOPER

Caring about others, running the risk of feeling, and leaving an impact on people, brings happiness.

>—**HAROLD KUSHNER**, RABBI

The older you get, the more you realize that kindness is synonymous with happiness.

>—**LIONEL BARRYMORE**, ACTOR

AFTER LOSING THE GAME

WHY DIDN'T YOU PASS THE BALL?!

I THOUGHT I'D TRY A 'QUARTER-BACK SNEAK'.

YOU WERE JUST SHOWING OFF.

NEXT WEEK, I'LL LET SOMEONE ELSE BE THE Q.B.!!

BEEP

BEEP

SUMTIMES BEIN' A TEAM PLYR MEANS SITTN ON TEH BENCH

HOW TO FORM AN
UNBEATABLE ALLIANCE
(WORKING WITH OTHERS)

Brett Favre is one of the greatest quarterbacks of all time. This is the guy who, after being smashed by three Steelers in a tough game, took a quick timeout, coughed up some blood, and raced back to throw a touchdown pass. He finished the division-clinching game with 301 yards.

But where would he be without his team? The coaches, the running backs, the wide receivers, the offensive guards, and the others work together to achieve victory. Even the water boy has a role in the team's success or failure. Brett Favre wouldn't have a place in sports history if it weren't for his team.

Think of all the things that require teams of people to cooperate and work toward a common goal. In your school, the teachers are important, but so are the bus drivers and cooks. You can't learn from your teacher if you aren't in your desk, and you can't focus on history if your stomach is growling all day. Even your family is a team. The adults pay the bills and manage the house, but the kids help with dishes, cooking, and cleaning.

Teams require a lot give and take. Everyone needs to do his or her share, and everyone has to compromise. Sometimes it seems like you're doing more work than your teammates, and it's not fair. Sometimes you feel guilty because you know you've been screwing around while everyone else has been giving 100 percent.

The accomplishments of a team make it worthwhile. When a team wins the game—or plays a perfect concert or turns in an awesome science project—you know you were part of something really cool.●

People who work together will win, whether it be against complex football defenses, or the problems of modern society.

—**VINCE LOMBARDI**, FOOTBALL COACH

Mötley Crüe is four individuals and that's what's kind of exciting. You have these four completely different characters that have four unique visions. When we're together, it equals one, but when we are separate, it equals four. It doesn't bother me. I think it's only good for the name Mötley Crüe.

—**NIKKI SIXX**, MUSICIAN

When you're directing, of course, you're supervising everything, but if you don't trust the artists you're collaborating with, you wind up tying one of their hands behind their back. My work got much, much better when I learned to let go a little bit.

—**RON HOWARD**, ACTOR AND FILM DIRECTOR INCLUDING *THE DAVINCI CODE*

We're one of those bands that turns into an animal when we feel that there's pressure. We hunker down and suck the marrow out of our bones for inspiration.

> —**TYSON RITTER**, BASSIST FOR ALL-
> AMERICAN REJECTS

If I have seen further than others, it is by standing upon the shoulders of giants.

> —**ISAAC NEWTON**, SCIENTIST

Talent wins games, but teamwork and intelligence win championships.

> —**MICHAEL JORDAN**, LEGENDARY FORMER
> BASKETBALL PLAYER FOR THE CHICAGO
> BULLS

In any band, you have a guy that jumps up and down and screams a lot, and then you will also have the one who just stands there.

> —**DAVE MATTHEWS**, MUSICIAN

We pray together and we have a time to focus and get ready. We call it lockdown, and we have 45 minutes where it's just us and no one comes in and no one goes out. It's a cool time to get focused and we just get psyched and really excited about the show.

—**JOE JONAS**, MUSICIAN AND MEMBER OF
THE JONAS BROTHERS

The people I've been running with, I've been running with for many, many, many years. I'm not a religious person, and I'm not too interested in being part of a religion, but I do like having some sort of communal gathering and having some sense of people.

—**IAN MACKAYE**, MUSICIAN AND MEMBER OF
FUGAZI

A team that has character doesn't need stimulation.

—**TOM LANDRY**, FOOTBALL PLAYER AND
COACH

The happiest people are those who are too busy to notice whether they are or not.

—**WILLIAM FEATHER**, PUBLISHER

To get the full value of a joy you must have some-body to divide it with.

—**MARK TWAIN**, HUMORIST AND WRITER

Affluence separates people. Poverty knits 'em together. You got some sugar and I don't; I borrow some of yours. Next month you might not have any flour; well, I'll give you some of mine

—**RAY CHARLES**, ACCLAIMED PIANIST AND
SOUL SINGER

There are two golden rules for an orchestra—start together and finish together. The public doesn't give a damn what goes on in between.

—**THOMAS BEECHAM**, CONDUCTOR

The greater the obstacle, the more glory in overcoming it.

—**MOLIERE**, FRENCH PLAYWRIGHT AND
ACTOR

None of us is as smart as all of us.

—**KEN BLANCHARD**, MANAGEMENT EXPERT

When someone does something good, applaud! You will make two people happy.

—**SAMUEL GOLDWYN**, AWARD-WINNING
PRODUCER

Family life is the source of the greatest human happiness.

—**ROBERT HAVIGHURST**, PHYSICIST AND
EDUCATOR

A life of frustration is inevitable for any coach whose main enjoyment is winning.

—**CHUCK NOLL**, FOOTBALL PLAYER AND
COACH

The English know how to make the best of things. Their so-called muddling through is simply skill at dealing with the inevitable.

—**WINSTON CHURCHILL**, BRITISH LEADER

Defensive strategy never has produced ultimate victory.

—**DOUGLAS MACARTHUR**, GENERAL

Being part of a team means that you take the bad with the team as well as taking the good with the team—that is the whole purpose.

— **MITCH GAYLORD**, OLYMPIC GYMNAST

I played because I enjoyed it, but there's more to it than that. I played because I was dedicated to being the best. I was part of a team, and I dedicated myself to making that team the best.

— **BILL RUSSELL**, BASKETBALL PLAYER

I'm going to do what I have to do, pat guys on the back, hug them, pick them up off the ground and hope they do the same for me and hope that's enough to win.

— **BRETT FAVRE**, FOOTBALL PLAYER AND THREE-TIME NFL MVP

My success wasn't based on how I could push down everybody that was around me. My success was based on how much I could push everybody up. And eventually their success was the same way. And in the process they pushed me up, and I pushed them up, and we kept doing that, and we still do that.

—**GEORGE LUCAS**, DIRECTOR AND CREATOR
OF *STAR WARS*

THE 20TH NINJA SECRET TO
BEING A TOTALLY UNSTOPPABLE KID

HOW TO BREAK
THROUGH ANY BARRIER

(CHALLENGING YOURSELF)

When it comes to soccer, you are the league master. You're the top scorer. You dribble around other players as if their bodies are made of stone. You're so fast you make David Beckham look like your grandfather's grandfather.

So maybe it's time to try piano or photography or choir.

Seriously.

It's great to have talent, and it's fun to be successful. But sometimes your success can keep you from trying new things. Maybe you've become so used to being the best that it feels risky to experiment with something different.

After all, it's not easy to go from expert soccer player to clunky pianist.

But it's cool take on a challenge. When things get too easy, you stop improving because you don't have to work very hard. You also risk growing an attitude bigger than your soccer field. Nobody wants to hang around a snob—even if you're a wickedly talented snob.

Trying something new revives your sense of excitement, the sense that absolutely anything could happen. Challenging activities make you set goals, learn more, and try harder. You're smarter, stronger, and sharper after you've tackled something that challenged your brain and body.

You don't have to give up doing the things you love. Nobody would tell a talented soccer player to dump his sport—unless he was truly bored with it. But adding something new to your life keeps you fresh. And chances are, you'll meet some cool people off the soccer field, too. ●

Somehow it's O.K. for people to chuckle about not being good at math. Yet if I said I never learned to read, they'd say I was an illiterate dolt. You can't look at science and math as separate. They're fundamental to what it is to be alive because they're all around us.

—**NEIL DEGRASSE TYSON,** SCIENTIST AND ASTROPHYSICIST

People who never get carried away should be.

—**MALCOLM FORBES,** AND PUBLISHER OF *FORBES* MAGAZINE

Baseball didn't really get into my blood until I knocked off that hitting streak. Getting a daily hit became more important to me than eating, drinking, or sleeping.

—**JOE DIMAGGIO,** BASEBALL PLAYER

The human spirit is stronger than anything that can happen to it.

—**GEORGE C. SCOTT,** ACTOR KNOWN FOR HIS ROLE IN DR. STRANGELOVE

I never was content unless I was trying my skill in some game against my fellow playmates or testing my endurance and wits against some member of the animal kingdom.

—**JIM THORPE**, FOOTBALL, BASEBALL PLAYER, AND TWO-TIME WINNER OF OLYMPIC GOLD MEDAL

For me, the hardest part is just staying on top of your game. It's easy to get pro, but hard to stay pro.

—**COLIN MCKAY**, PROFESSIONAL SKATEBOARDER

It's really nice to be able to do something that you've never done. I think that's the gift of being an actor because I get to play a cop . . . and I've never done that before.

—**MATT DAMON**, ACTOR BEST KNOWN FOR WRITING, DIRECTING, AND STARRING IN *GOOD WILL HUNTING*

In times of stress, be bold and valiant.

—**HORACE**, POET

Facing it—always facing it—that's the way to get through. Face it!

—JOSEPH CONRAD, WRITER

I never intended to become an author—writing *Eragon* was just a wild challenge for myself, an attempt to produce a book-length work, without any intention of publishing it.

—CHRISTOPHER PAOLINI, FANTASY WRITER

I was full of pie, ice cream, and inexperience. To me, golf was just a game to beat someone. I didn't know that someone was me.

—BOBBY JONES, GOLFER INDUCTED INTO THE WORLD GOLF HALL OF FAME

Bravery and faith bring both material and spiritual rewards.

—PRESTON BRADLEY, MINISTER

There is something healthy and invigorating about direct action.

—HENRY MILLER, WRITER

All problems become smaller if you don't dodge them, but confront them.

> —WILLIAM F. HALSEY, NAVAL OFFICER

Get in front of the ball, you won't get hurt. That's what you've got a chest for, young man.

> —JOHN MCGRAW, BASEBALL PLAYER AND
> MANAGER

The test of courage comes when we are in the minority.

> —RALPH W. SOCKMAN, MINISTER

It takes vision and courage to create—it takes faith and courage to prove.

> —OWEN D. YOUNG, BUSINESSMAN

If you get to a point where you don't feel you can make any improvements, then you're going downhill because there's somebody out there who's making improvements.

> —RICK SWENSON, IDITAROD COMPETITOR

What would life be if we had no courage to attempt anything?

—**VINCENT VAN GOGH**, EXPRESSIONIST PAINTER

In every aspect the White Stripes is a band that has no safety nets. There's no set lists. Meg and I hardly ever rehearse for a tour or a live show. My guitars aren't very well made, like kids' first guitars, and maybe people don't know that it's harder to play—it's important to me that there's a struggle happening.

—**JACK WHITE**, MUSICIAN

Courage is being scared to death . . . and saddling up anyway.

—**JOHN WAYNE**, AWARD-WINNING ACTOR

Preparation for tours is the toughest bit for me. Rehearsals—you have to time your day and time your body. It's hard, physically.

—**MICK JAGGER**, MUSICIAN AND FRONTMAN FOR THE ROLLING STONES

HOW TO LEAD A TEAM OF DO-GOODERS

(BEING A ROLE MODEL)

You know that pesky neighbor kid who's always hanging around? The one with the runny nose who constantly tells those stupid knock-knock jokes? Like it or not, you're probably his role model. He wouldn't be following you around so he can tell his jokes if he didn't look up to you.

You may also find yourself a role model to boys your own age. They might look up to you because you're a talented artist, because you stand up to bullies or because you're smart. Whether your biggest fan is the pesky six-year-old from next door or the guy who sits next to you in math class, being a role model is a big responsibility—even if you didn't ask for it.

Here are a few ways to think about it:

Be nice, even when you're tempted to be a wiseguy. It's easy to let admiration go to your head, and it's very easy to get annoyed by the knock-knock joke kid. But remember: It hurts when people are mean to you, and it *really* hurts when the people you *like* are mean to you.

Be an example. The kids who admire you learn from what you say, but they learn even more from what you do.

Just because someone looks up to you doesn't mean you're suddenly a counselor. Be a good listener, but encourage people to work out their own problems.

As your fans grow up, they'll eventually find other role models, so enjoy your devoted following while it lasts. And, no doubt, your fan club will gain a batch of new members to replace them.●

Playing guru is a tricky business. I realized that I had an ability to inspire and help other artists without influencing their style or hurting their own personal integrity. The most valuable thing an artist possesses is his or her personal integrity. I like to protect that in others.

—**ROBERT GENN**, PAINTER

This is a role model. Don't be like me.

—**MICKEY MANTLE**, BASEBALL PLAYER AND HOMERUN RECORD HOLDER

A life is not important except in the impact it has on other lives.

—**JACKIE ROBINSON**, FIRST AFRICAN AMERICAN MAJOR LEAGUE BASEBALL PLAYER

When people are free to do as they please, they usually imitate each other.

—**ERIC HOFFER**, PHILOSOPHER

If you are given a chance to be a role model, I think you should always take it because you can influence a person's life in a positive light, and that's what I want to do. That's what it's all about.

—**TIGER WOODS**, GOLFER OFTEN CONSIDERED BEST IN HISTORY OF THE SPORT

Example is not the main thing in influencing others. It is the only thing.

—**ALBERT SCHWEITZER**, PHILOSOPHER AND THEOLOGIAN

Nothing is so infectious as example.

—**FRANCOIS DE LA ROCHEFOUCAULD**, WRITER

I want to be remembered as a strong and graceful diver. But as a person, I want to be remembered as someone who made a difference.

—**GREG LOUGANIS**, OLYMPIC DIVER

Show me a successful individual and I'll show you someone who had real positive influences in his or her life.

—**DENZEL WASHINGTON**, AWARD-WINNING ACTOR AND STAR OF *TRAINING DAY*

People seldom improve when they have no other model but themselves to copy.

—**OLIVER GOLDSMITH**, WRITER AND PHYSICIAN

Example moves the world more than doctrine.

—**HENRY MILLER**, WRITER

Wise men learn by other men's mistakes, fools by their own.

—**H.G. BOHN**, PUBLISHER

I don't believe professional athletes should be role models. I believe parents should be role models.

—**CHARLES BARKLEY**, BASKETBALL PLAYER AND NBA MVP

Leaders are visionaries with a poorly developed sense of fear and no concept of the odds against them. They make the impossible happen.

—**ROBERT JARVIK**, RESEARCHER

As you get older, it is harder to have heroes, but it is sort of necessary.

—**ERNEST HEMINGWAY**, WRITER AND
WINNER OF THE NOBEL PRIZE

We take pride in helping make talented people better. It's a matter of good stewardship, passing on the gifts God has given us.

—**JEFF DANIELS**, ACTOR

A good meal is only as good as those who make it.

—**ALTON BROWN**, CHEF AND STAR OF
GOOD EATS

Without heroes, we are all plain people and don't know how far we can go.

—**BERNARD MALAMUD**, WRITER

Celebrity is currency, so I wanted to use mine effectively.

—**BONO**, LEAD SINGER OF U2

That Elvis, man, he is all there is. There ain't no more. Everything starts and ends with him. He wrote the book.

—**BRUCE SPRINGSTEEN**, MUSICIAN AND
FRONTMAN FOR THE E STREET BAND

I don't have to look anywhere for inspiration or for reasons to get out of bed and work my ass off. What I do is easy compared to what my family has always done.

—**MATT STILLWELL**, COUNTRY MUSICIAN

As a mature adult, I feel an obligation to help the younger generation, just as the mother fish guards her unhatched eggs, keeping her lonely vigil day after day, never leaving her post, not even to go to the bathroom, until her tiny babies emerge and she is able, at last, to eat them.

—**DAVE BARRY**, HUMORIST

WHATCHA WORKING ON?

A WEBSITE FOR MY DAD'S COMPANY.

FUN!

IT'S ABOUT *PLUMBING.* ÜBER-BORING!

PLUMBING SUPPLIES

60% OFF

BUT IT MIGHT EARN YOU EXTRA CREDIT IN DESIGN CLASS.

GUESS I NEVER THOUGHT OF *THAT*.

OOPS, HANG ON...

I'M GETTING AN I.M.

PING

60% OFF

You have a new message!

Ninja22

Ninja22: OPPRTNTIES R USLLY DISGIZED AS HRD WRK. THTS WHY U DONT ALWYS RCGNZ THM!

HOW TO FIND HIDDEN PASSAGEWAYS

(LOOKING FOR OPPORTUNITIES)

So you want to be a rock star? The obvious first step is to learn how to wail on an instrument like guitar or drums. But there are also hidden doors to your dream all over the place—you just need to look for them.

Your place of worship might not seem like a gateway to rock-and-roll, but joining the church choir can teach you about melodies, singing with a group, and hitting the right notes. And the poetry segment in English class can help you understand how words are strung together in ways that make cool lyrics. If you fail to see these everyday moments as opportunities, you're missing chances to get closer to your dream.

Ask some adults you know about jobs they hated or considered a road to nowhere. That first job serving burgers and French fries was hard, sweaty work serving mean customers and getting a tiny paycheck. But maybe the job led to meeting a lifelong best friend, learning how to live on a budget, or moving to New York to become a real chef in a fancy restaurant. All the time they spent asking customers, "Do you want fries with that?" turned out to experience for their life's next big adventure.

Think about what you want to do in the years ahead: a cool part-time job at a bike store, getting on the starting lineup of a sports team, or getting paid to design websites. Then start living each and every day like you're a detective searching for opportunities that could lead to your goals. Remember, the passageways to your dreams might be hiding in some strange places.●

We're always fighting a battle to improve ourselves at something, and right now, this moment, is another opportunity to turn it around.

    —**TONY ROMO**, FOOTBALL PLAYER

I always tried to turn every disaster into an opportunity.

    —**JOHN D. ROCKEFELLER**, BUSINESSMAN

Start where you are. Use what you have. Do what you can.

    —**ARTHUR ASHE**, TENNIS PLAYER

I devoured records. I could feel the magic of being in front of an audience, just by listening to these masters. I learned about timing by listening to the way the comic would wait for the laugh to die down, and then hit the crowd with the topper. It was like surfing, riding the wave, and taking it wherever it was going.

    —**BILLY CRYSTAL**, COMEDIAN, ACTOR, AND
       STAR OF *WHEN HARRY MET SALLY*

My wife says that the best way to describe my life is Forrest Gump. I find myself surrounded by extraordinary people that give me unusual opportunities, so I do the best I can.

—**RODNEY MULLEN**, PROFESSIONAL SKATEBOARDER

Opportunity is like a bald-headed man with only a patch of hair right in front. You have to grab that hair, grasp the opportunity while it's confronting you, or else you'll be grasping a slick bald head.

—**BOOKER T. WASHINGTON**, EDUCATOR AND POLITICAL LEADER

If you prepare, then the opportunities will take care of themselves.

—**JOHN O'HURLEY**, ACTOR AND HOST OF *FAMILY FEUD*

I think the young actor who really wants to act will find a way . . . to keep at it and seize every opportunity that comes along.

—**JOHN GIELGUD**, AWARD-WINNING ACTOR

The successful man is one who had the chance and took it.

—**ROGER BABSON**, ENTREPRENEUR

It is often hard to distinguish between the hard knocks in life and those of opportunity.

—**FREDERICK PHILLIPS**, HOCKEY PLAYER

We must look for the opportunity in every difficulty instead of being paralyzed at the thought of the difficulty in every opportunity.

—**WALTER E. COLE**, IRISH POLITICIAN

Opportunity is missed by most people because it is dressed in overalls and looks like work.

—**THOMAS EDISON**, INVENTOR

Every day is a new opportunity. You can build on yesterday's success or put its failures behind and start over again. That's the way life is, with a new game every day, and that's the way baseball is.

—**BOB FELLER**, BASEBALL PLAYER

A filly who wants to run will always find a rider.

    —JACQUES AUDIBERTI, WRITER

Use only that which works, and take it from any place you can find it.

    —BRUCE LEE, LEGENDARY MARTIAL ARTIST,
       ACTOR, AND FOUNDER OF JEET KUNE DO
       COMBAT

Mediocre men wait for opportunity to come to them. Strong, able, alert men go after opportunity.

    —B. C. FORBES, PUBLISHER

There is no security on this earth. Only opportunity.

    —DOUGLAS MACARTHUR, GENERAL

You decide you'll wait for your pitch. Then as the ball starts toward the plate, you think about your stance. And then you think about your swing. And then you realize that the ball that went past you for a strike was your pitch.

    —BOBBY MURCER, BASEBALL PLAYER

Every man is the architect of his own fortune.

> —**SALLUST**, ROMAN HISTORIAN

I grew up with six brothers. That's how I learned to dance—waiting for the bathroom.

> —**BOB HOPE**, COMEDIAN AND ACTOR

Our opportunities to do good are our talents.

> —**COTTON MATHER**, WRITER AND MINISTER

I wasn't driven to acting by any inner compulsion. I was running away from the sporting goods business.

> —**PAUL NEWMAN**, ACTOR

The secret to success in life is for a man to be ready for his opportunity when it comes.

> —**BENJAMIN DISRAELI**, BRITISH POLITICIAN

Yesterday ended last night. Every day is a new beginning. Learn the skill of forgetting. And move on.

> —**NORMAN VINCENT PEALE**, MINISTER AND WRITER

WHERE TO GO WHEN YOUR LUCK RUNS OUT

(MAKING YOUR OWN LUCK)

Some people act like everything in life just happens. Something goes wrong? Darn—it's bad luck! Something goes right? Rock on—it's good luck! But the people who connect a direct line between luck and success are giving up the remote control to their lives.

Luck is not this mystical force that flows through the galaxy, touching some people while ignoring others. People make their own luck by planning, working hard and finding opportunities. Their final destination may appear to be good luck, but if you watched the journey closely, you'll see how hard they worked along the way.

You can make your own luck, too. Here's how:

Know what it is you want. It's hard to "get lucky" if you haven't thought about your goals. Do you want better grades? A puppy for the family? A new snowboard? First place in a relay?

Break down your goal into small steps. If you want that snowboard, start mowing lawns in the summer to earn the money. Then do research to learn about the best snowboards and find the best prices.

Celebrate your progress, but don't get discouraged if your plans don't always work out. It doesn't mean you're unlucky or that you messed up! You probably need to change your plan.

If you're waiting for a lucky day, you could be waiting until your hair turns gray. Your dreams are possible, but you won't achieve them through sheer luck. Good fortune is everywhere—you just have to use your brains, develop a positive attitude and keep trying despite the setbacks. ●

I was very, very inexplicably lucky. But it's more than luck. Luck comes as a result of some other energies.

> —**SIDNEY POITIER**, AWARD-WINNING ACTOR

The successful man is one who had the chance and took it.

> —**ROGER BABSON**, ENTREPRENEUR AND FOUNDER OF BABSON COLLEGE

Winners are men who have dedicated their whole lives to winning.

> —**WOODY HAYES**, FOOTBALL COACH

The person who makes a success of living is the one who sees his goal steadily and aims for it unswervingly. That is dedication.

> —**CECIL B. DEMILLE**, AWARD-WINNING FILM DIRECTOR

The wise man puts all his eggs in one basket and watches the basket.

> —**ANDREW CARNEGIE**, STEEL BARON AND PHILANTHROPIST

I didn't know what it was going to be, but I knew that I was going to take advantage of it when I got the chance.

  —**TIM MCGRAW**, COUNTRY MUSICIAN

The champion makes his own luck.

  —**RED BLAIK**, FOOTBALL COACH

Great minds have purposes, others have wishes.

  —**WASHINGTON IRVING**, WRITER AND
   HISTORIAN

I realized that if my passion for something I loved and was good at was starting to wane, then maybe there was something else I was supposed to do.

  —**JOE MOGLIA**, BUSINESSMAN

All of my life, I have been fascinated by the big questions that face us, and have tried to find scientific answers to them. Perhaps that is why I have sold more books on physics than Madonna has on sex.

  —**STEPHEN HAWKING**, PHYSICIST

You can't try to do things; you simply must do them.

—**RAY BRADBURY**, AUTHOR OF
FAHRENHEIT 451

Luck is the by-product of busting your fanny.

—**DON SUTTON**, BASEBALL PLAYER AND
BROADCASTER

Sometimes success is due less to ability than zeal.
The winner is he who gives himself to his work body
and soul.

—**CHARLES BUXTON**, PHILANTHROPIST

The only sure thing about luck is that it will change.

—**BRET HARTE**, WRITER

The harder I practice, the luckier I get.

—**GARY PLAYER**, GOLFER AND MEMBER OF
THE WORLD GOLF HALL OF FAME

Motivation triggers luck.

—**MIKE WALLACE**, JOURNALIST KNOWN FOR
REPORTING ON *60 MINUTES*

The first time that I appeared on stage, it scared me to death. I really didn't know what all the yelling was about. I didn't realize that my body was moving. It's a natural thing to me. So to the manager backstage I said, "What'd I do? What'd I do?" And he said, "Whatever it is, go back and do it again."

—**ELVIS PRESLEY**, MUSICIAN

Get as much experience as you can, so that you're ready when luck works. That's the luck.

—**HENRY FONDA**, ACTOR

I'm always pushing myself. I don't need external motivation to try to move things along.

—**TOBY KEITH**, COUNTRY MUSICIAN

The pool in Athens was supposed to have a roof. It didn't. People still swam fast. People still competed. It's the Olympic Games. You can't make an excuse about the Olympic Games. Either you're ready or you're not.

—**MICHAEL PHELPS**, OLYMPIC SWIMMER AND GOLD MEDAL WINNER

There's a lot to being young and stupid. There's a vitality to that. If you actually had waited a few years and developed common sense you probably wouldn't do it, but you're so young you think, "I can do this. It's no big deal."

—ERIC CHURCH, COUNTRY MUSICIAN

Work with patience and perseverance and you are sure to find some measure of satisfaction.

—MAS OYAMA, KARATE MASTER

I've found that luck is quite predictable. If you want more luck, take more chances. Be more active. Show up more often.

—BRIAN TRACY, SELF-HELP WRITER

I watched friends do showcases and hope someone would show up. I watched them being promised record or publishing deals that might or might not happen. So I made the decision that what I needed to do was to eliminate the no's, and the way to do that was to go build a following.

—MATT STILLWELL, COUNTRY MUSICIAN

HOW DO NINJAS BECOME INVISIBLE?

IT'S A TRICK THAT REQUIRES HARD WORK.

I'LL SHOW YOU.

GO INTO THE BROOM CLOSET.

CLICK

WHAT DOES THIS HAVE TO DO WITH INVISIBILITY?

CAN YOU SEE ME EATING YOUR LUNCH?

WELL... NO.

SEE? I WORKED HARD AT MASTERING THAT TRICK

THE 24TH NINJA SECRET TO BEING A TOTALLY UNSTOPPABLE KID

HOW TO ACCOMPLISH ANY MISSION

(HARD WORK)

Work is the thing that gets you from mission impossible to mission accomplished. Whether it's school, sports, games, or art, hard work is the key if you're serious about doing your best.

The funny thing about work is it's one of those chameleon words that has a different meaning depending on who's using it. If you're used to lots of couch-and-TV time, then shoveling a long driveway after a blizzard is back-breaking work. If you're a guy who benches 200 pounds after two hours of working out, you might think writing a book report is a complete brain drain. And if you hated finger painting even in kindergarten, you probably get stressed out when your teacher assigns an art project.

Working hard is probably not on your top-ten list of fun things to do, but your efforts are often rewarded with a big pay-off: first place in the school science fair, a solo in the choir concert, or a paycheck to buy the football jersey you've wanted all year.

People notice those efforts, too. You win their admiration by setting your sights on a goal and working to earn it. High-fives will follow!

But working hard has another reward, too—one that you can't see, smell, or touch. It's that sense of pride you get when you've done your best, even if you didn't win a blue ribbon or land the concert solo. Money can't buy a feeling like that, and there aren't enough compliments in the world to make you feel it if you didn't earn it. The price tag for pride is your best effort.

When I make music, it has to mean something to me. Some people are like, "You take yourself so seriously." Well, would you rather I don't take what I do seriously?

—**DJ SHADOW**, MUSICIAN

If you start to take Vienna, take Vienna.

—**NAPOLEON BONAPARTE**, FRENCH LEADER

And I have to say after fifteen years, the kind of comic I dreamed about being, I'm there. I still have a lot of work to do, and I feel like it's a work in progress.

—**DANE COOK**, COMEDIAN, ACTOR, AND
STAR OF *GOOD LUCK CHUCK*

I never had a sore arm, and I pitched every third day. Once I pitched every other day for 18 days.

—**CY YOUNG**, BASEBALL PLAYER

What one has, one ought to use; and whatever he does, he should do with all his might.

—**CICERO**, PHILOSOPHER

There's no labor a man can do that's undignified, if he does it right.

—**BILL COSBY**, ACTOR AND COMEDIAN

The road to happiness lies in two simple principles: find what it is that interests you and that you can do well, and when you find it, put your whole soul into it—every bit of energy and ambition and natural ability you have.

—**JOHN D. ROCKEFELLER III**, PHILANTHROPIST

The happy people are those who are producing something.

—**WILLIAM RALPH INGE**, PROFESSOR AND WRITER

I had no natural gift to be anything—not an athlete, not an actor, not a writer, not a director, a painter of garden porches—not anything. So I've worked really hard, because nothing ever came easily to me.

—**PAUL NEWMAN**, ACTOR AND STAR OF *COOL HAND LUKE*

You can't overstate the value of setting a goal for yourself and achieving it.

> —**SEAN ASTIN**, ACTOR WHO STARRED IN *THE GOONIES*

You have to work extremely hard to be successful, and that never ends. People think if you're a successful writer, writing eventually comes easier to you. In fact, in many ways it means it's even harder. No matter what field you're in, you want to make sure your work is growing, evolving.

> —**MALCOLM GLADWELL**, WRITER AND *NEW YORK TIMES* BESTSELLING AUTHOR

The highest reward for man's toil is not what he gets for it, but what he becomes by it.

> —**JOHN RUSKIN**, ART CRITIC

Do your best work. Work as hard as you can on any given day and try to live it down.

> —**DAVID FINCHER**, FILM DIRECTOR OF *SEVEN* AND *FIGHT CLUB*

I get satisfaction of three kinds. One is creating something, one is being paid for it, and one is the feeling that I haven't just been sitting on my ass all afternoon.

> —**WILLIAM F. BUCKLEY**, WRITER AND COMMENTATOR

I mean it all revolves around skateboarding. Everything I'm doing is to be a better skateboarder.

> —**BOB BURNQUIST**, PROFESSIONAL SKATEBOARDER

The first moment we think we're favorites and we're going to win easily, that's when we are going to feel it and we are going to struggle.

> —**SERGIO GARCIA**, GOLFER

I put the same amount of heart and soul into a 100-million-dollar movie as I do a 3-million-dollar movie. You have to. You can't just deliver your performance based on the size of the budget.

> —**KEVIN BACON**, ACTOR AND STAR OF *FOOTLOOSE*

The more I want to get something done, the less I call it work.

    —**RICHARD BACH**, WRITER

Honest labor bears a lovely face.

    —**THOMAS DEKKER**, POET

Love what you do. Get good at it. Competence is a rare commodity in this day and age. And let the chips fall where they may.

    —**JON STEWART**, COMEDIAN AND TALK
    SHOW SHOT

Success usually comes to those who are too busy to be looking for it.

    —**HENRY DAVID THOREAU**, PHILOSOPHER

Any talented kid can go to Breckenridge and hit the big 80-foot kickers. But it's the struggle of surviving in the backcountry that gets the respect of your peers.

    —**KEIR DILLON**, PROFESSIONAL
    SNOWBOARDER

SPARRING PRACTICE

WHOOSH!!

SHA!

POKE

YOU WERE RIGHT!

IF I JUST KEPT TRYING... I'D EVENTUALLY GET YOU IN *THE END!*

HOW TO BE THE
LAST MAN STANDING

(PERSEVERANCE)

Sometimes you'll need to turn to family and friends for inspiration and advice, but there's actually a better role model: Krazy Glue®. That's because when you're struggling to finish a school project or a list of chores, you need to learn the glue-like skill of refusing to quit.

It's tempting to give up when something is hard or you don't like doing it. Let's say you've been struggling to finish a book report while your friend nailed it in one night. It's frustrating to see how easy writing is for Mr. English. You might be tempted to crank out a mess of words and hand the assignment to your teacher, even though it's not your best work.

But it's important to stop comparing yourself to other people. Because no matter how hard you work, there is always going to be somebody who's a better writer, a stronger climber, a faster cyclist.

Here are some ideas to help you stick with it:

- Plan a reward for yourself when you finish the job. It'll help you stay motivated.

- Don't force yourself to follow a crazy schedule. It's better to do something well than to do it fast.

- Ask other people what tricks they use to stay focused on things that are tough. You'll learn some good tips, and you'll probably find out that Mr. English works harder than you ever thought.

When you refuse to quit, you'll see that you can accomplish almost anything. ●

That's the key: being able to take humiliation when people say, "Why are you doing this, you are a fool, you're an idiot." And you carry on through it.

—**EDDIE IZZARD**, COMEDIAN

When I'm focused, there is not one single thing, person, anything that can stand in my way of doing something. There is not. Never has been. If I want something bad enough, then I'm gonna get there.

—**MICHAEL PHELPS**, OLYMPIC SWIMMER AND GOLD MEDAL WINNER

I lived in my car for a long time. Plenty of nights I cried because I thought we'd go out of business. But when you have this dream and you love what you do, you do it.

—**TOM SCOTT**, BUSINESSMAN

When it goes wrong, you feel like cutting your throat, but you go on. You don't let anything get you down so much that it beats you or stops you.

—**GEORGE CUKOR**, AWARD-WINNING FILM DIRECTOR

We conquer by continuing.

 —**GEORGE MATHESON**, THEOLOGIAN

There's nothing in this world that comes easy. There are a lot of people who aren't going to bother to win. We learn in football to get up and go once more.

 —**WOODY HAYES**, FOOTBALL COACH

To persevere, trusting in what hopes he has, is courage in a man. The coward despairs.

 —**EURIPIDES**, PLAYWRIGHT

I realized early on that success was tied to not giving up. Most people in this business gave up and went on to other things. If you simply didn't give up, you would outlast the people who came in on the bus with you.

 —**HARRISON FORD**, STAR OF THE *INDIANA JONES* MOVIES

Everything must have a beginning, and great things cannot be accomplished in a handful of days.

 —**MAS OYAMA**, KARATE MASTER

I've never been one for scratching. I don't believe in it. I think it takes something away from the race if you're going to pick up your ball and go home. It says something to stick it out.

> —**DEWEY HALVERSON**, IDITAROD
> COMPETITOR

The Smashing Pumpkins was never meant to be a small band. It was going to either be a big band, or no band.

> —**BILLY CORGAN**, MUSICIAN AND FRONTMAN
> FOR THE SMASHING PUMPKINS

Everything's relative; no one gets to corner the market on misery.

> —**CHRISTOPHER REEVES**, ACTOR, ACTIVIST,
> AND STAR OF *SUPERMAN*

I know the price of success: dedication, hard work, and an unremitting devotion to the things you want to see happen.

> —**FRANK LLOYD WRIGHT**, ARCHITECT

Big shots are only little shots who keep shooting.

—**CHRISTOPHER MORLEY**, WRITER

There's such a thin line between winning and losing.

—**JOHN R. TUNIS**, WRITER

You give 100 percent in the first half of the game, and if that isn't enough, in the second half you give what's left.

—**YOGI BERRA**, BASEBALL COACH AND
THREE-TIME AMERICAN LEAGUE MVP

If something doesn't come up the way you want, you have to forge ahead.

—**CLINT EASTWOOD**, AWARD-WINNING
ACTOR, DIRECTOR, AND ANTI-HERO

I've always been like a boomerang. You can throw me away, but you can rest assured that I'm coming back.

—**KENNY ROGERS**, COUNTRY MUSIC SINGER
AND SONGWRITER

The tragedy of life is not that man loses, but that he almost wins.

—**HEYWOOD BROUN**, JOURNALIST

Saints are sinners who kept on going.

—**ROBERT LOUIS STEVENSON**, WRITER

Interception, a loss, you name it. You deal with it. You learn from it. You address it, and it's hard to get over, especially a loss. It is hard.

—**PEYTON MANNING**, FOOTBALL PLAYER AND THREE-TIME NFL MVP

I find it deeply tragic when great ideas lie in the minds of people who think that everybody else's ideas are better. What a different world it would be if people accomplished all of the great things they would like to do! What you verbalize to yourself you must complete. I believe that.

—**JOHN O'HURLEY**, ACTOR AND HOST OF *FAMILY FEUD*

WHOOP

WHOOP

WATCH...
TWO AT
ONCE!

WHOOP

WHOOP

WHOOP

WHOOP

BONK

DON'T
FEEL
BAD...

I HEAR
THAT EVEN
HAPPENED
TO BRUCE
LEE, ONCE!

RECOVERING FROM A FAILED MISSION

(LEARNING FROM MISTAKES)

A mistake is only a genuine mistake if you repeat it. Think about that for a minute. Life's little lesson book is built on mistakes. Messing up is how you grow, learn, and succeed.

Consider this: There are ten seconds left in the football game, and you're the quarterback. You have two options. You can pass the ball to a receiver, who's wide open in the endzone, or try to run the ball in yourself. If you can make it past the defensive line, you're the season's superstar. So you go for the sneak. And you get creamed at the line of scrimmage.

Definitely the wrong call. But you learned something: Don't let your pride get in the way of making the right play for the team. You'll be a better player in the future because of the experience. It's only a real mistake if you act like a ball hog again during the next game.

If you really messed up, here are some tips for a smooth recovery:

If you hurt somebody's feelings, admit what you did and say you're sorry. That takes guts, and people will admire your courage.

Think about the situation. What led to the mistake? How can you stop it from happening again?

Don't get all "emo" about it. Everyone screws up. What's important is learning from your mistakes.

Learn to laugh at yourself. Later—sometimes *much* later—those mistakes make some interesting stories.

Making the wrong move from time to time proves that you're not just *breathing*, you're actually *living*. Mistakes can be downright embarrassing. But remember, if you learn and grow, a mistake is a gift in disguise.●

Seize every opportunity you have to learn. Keep your eyes and ears wide open and seize life—don't let the moments slip through your fingers like a fistful of sand.

—**RICHIE SAMBORA**, MUSICIAN AND LEAD GUITARIST OF BON JOVI

We're on the quest for the perfect performance and every note has to be right. Man, every note is not right in life. There are bumps in the road and misses and squeaks.

—**BRANFORD MARSALIS**, SAXOPHONIST AND COMPOSER

Success is a lousy teacher. It seduces smart people into thinking they can't lose.

—**BILL GATES**, FOUNDER OF MICROSOFT, MULTIBILLIONAIRE, AND PHILANTHROPIST

How you carry yourself in this world, unfortunately, is how you get labeled. That's just the way it is: you get labeled.

—**LUKE CAMPBELL**, RAPPER AND LEADER OF 2 LIVE CREW

An act like ours wouldn't even be around today if someone hadn't brought us along and let us make mistakes and grow at our own pace. Today it seems that if you don't have a hit—or even if you do—they have no use for you the next time.

—**TOM PETTY,** MUSICIAN AND FRONTMAN
FOR TOM PETTY AND THE HEARTBREAKERS

Those who make no mistakes are making the biggest mistakes of all—they are attempting nothing new.

—**ANTHONY DE MELLO,** PRIEST AND WRITER

When I had my own sons, I was young, and I was involved with me, and I missed what I should have done in their formative years. Now I am making up for as much as I can.

—**JERRY LEWIS,** COMEDIAN

The best we can do is open our hearts and learn to appreciate and forgive.

—**ADRIAN GRENIER,** ACTOR STARRING IN
ENTOURAGE

Experience is the name everyone gives to their mistakes.

—OSCAR WILDE, NOVELIST AND
   PLAYWRIGHT

I like a man with faults, especially when he knows it. To err is human—I'm uncomfortable around gods.

—HUGH PRATHER, MINISTER AND WRITER

Striving for perfection is the greatest stopper there is. You'll be afraid you can't achieve it. . . . It's your excuse to yourself for not doing anything. Instead, strive for excellence, doing your best.

—SIR LAURENCE OLIVER, ACTOR

What, after all, is a halo? It's only one more thing to keep clean.

—CHRISTOPHER FRY, PLAYWRIGHT

We don't spend much time dwelling on things gone right. But we do take things apart, and for the missed opportunities and for the missteps, we agonize over it and we commit not to have those things reoccur.

—**JACK ROUSH**, RACE CAR DRIVER

All of us failed to match our dreams of perfection.

—**WILLIAM FAULKNER**, WRITER AND WINNER
    OF THE NOBEL PRIZE

I only have to stop the puck, not beat it to death.

—**DON BEAUPRE**, HOCKEY PLAYER

Perfectionism is a dangerous state of mind in an imperfect world.

—**ROBERT HILLYER**, POET

You build on failure. You use it as a stepping stone. Close the door on the past. You don't try to forget the mistakes, but you don't dwell on it. You don't let it have any of your energy, or any of your time, or any of your space.

—**JOHNNY CASH**, MUSICIAN

When I was young and crazy, I was young and crazy. It can be hard enough just to BE in your teens and 20s. Then add fame, money, access, and every single person telling you that you're the greatest person who ever was, and it can be a recipe for disaster. Some people literally don't survive it.

—ROB LOWE, ACTOR STARRING IN
ST. ELMO'S FIRE

The artist who aims at perfection in everything achieves it in nothing.

—EUGENE DELACROIX, ARTIST

A man would do nothing if he waited until he could do it so well that no one could find fault.

—JOHN HENRY CARDINAL NEWMAN, PRIEST

When I make mistakes, I know I've got to step back, and instead of pounding myself for it, I just go. Listen, man, I'm in it—I'm in the ring. Sometimes you've just got to run with your mistakes.

—BRAD PITT, AWARD-WINNING ACTOR AND
PRODUCER

THE 27TH NINJA SECRET TO BEING A TOTALLY UNSTOPPABLE KID

HOW TO DIFFUSE A STRESS BOMB

(ANXIETY AND ANGER MANAGEMENT)

Back when humans lived in caves and hunted with sticks, stress was a lifesaver. Those who felt stress knew exactly when to run, hide and fight. Those who didn't . . . well, they were easy meals for hungry lions.

Today, stress is still natural—and often a good thing. Stress often gives you the extra edge you need to accomplish something difficult or nerve-wracking. If you feel stressed about a math test, you're going to study harder. You get a boost of energy from stress right before a soccer game.

But sometimes stress doesn't know when to back off. If your stomach hurts, if you can't sleep, or if you feel tense and worried, you've gone past stress territory and into the land of anxiety. That's not a good thing. Anxiety makes it difficult to get through the day. It's like worrying, but at warp speed.

Here are some ways to deal with anxiety:

- Try something relaxing: hang out in a tree fort, read a graphic novel, or watch a no-brain TV show that makes you laugh.

- Talk to people you trust. Sometimes just describing your anxiety helps soften the edge.

- Get some air in your lungs. Your body will release stress when you get some exercise. Choose a high-intensity activity like running, biking, or swimming.

If nothing seems to be helping, you need to talk to your parents or a school counselor. Sometimes people need professional help to deal with anxiety. It's important to tackle the problem before it gets too big. ●

Sometimes, getting up in the morning and brushing your teeth is the hardest part of the day—it all just hurts.

—TOM BRADY, FOOTBALL PLAYER

If I can handle my stress, that tells me I've done what I needed to. If I can't handle it, I know next time, I have to be better prepared.

—HERM EDWARDS, FOOTBALL COACH

For as long as I can remember I have suffered from a deep feeling of anxiety which I have tried to express in my art. Without anxiety and illness I should have been like a ship without a rudder.

—EDVARD MUNCH, ARTIST BEST KNOWN FOR *THE SCREAM*

When you're a professional, you come back no matter what happened the day before.

—BILLY MARTIN, BASEBALL PLAYER

You know more than you think you do.

—BENJAMIN SPOCK, PHYSICIAN AND AUTHOR

223

I used to be a real prince charming if I went on a date with a girl. But then I'd get to where I was likely to have a stroke from the stress of keeping up my act. I've since learned the key to a good date is to pay attention on her.

    —**MATTHEW PERRY**, ACTOR STARRING ON
       FRIENDS

You can overcome anything if you don't bellyache.

    —**BERNARD M. BARUCH**, BUSINESSMAN

All problems become smaller if you don't dodge them, but confront them.

    —**WILLIAM F. HALSEY**, NAVAL COMMANDER

Good people are good because they've come to wisdom through failure.

    —**WILLIAM SAROYAN**, WRITER

Fight one more round. When your feet are so tired you have to shuffle back to the center of the ring, fight one more round.

    —**JAMES CORBETT**, WRITER

The first and final thing you have to do in this world is to last in it, and not be smashed by it.

—**ERNEST HEMINGWAY**, WRITER AND
WINNER OF THE NOBEL PRIZE

If you actively do something, it will stop making you feel like a victim and you'll start feeling like part of the solution, which is just a huge benefit to your body and your psyche.

—**TED DANSON**, ACTOR STARRING IN *CHEERS*

Real difficulties can be overcome, it is only the imaginary ones that are unconquerable.

—**THEODORE N. VAIL**, ENTREPRENEUR

You can get through some real tough moments with that guitar on your knee. When life gets intense, there are people who drink, who seek counseling, eat, or watch TV, pray, cry, sleep, and so on. I play.

—**BRAD PAISLEY**, COUNTRY MUSICIAN

Inches make a champion.

—**VINCE LOMBARDI**, FOOTBALL COACH

Somehow the usual anxieties of life—money, status, the possibility of a meteorite landing on my head—didn't matter when every atom of my humanity was focused on mastering the four-fingered D chord. Experts in positive psychology call it flow, the rosy feeling of losing oneself in a challenging activity.

—**DAVID HOCHMAN**, MUSICIAN

If you have a football and 11 guys are after you, if you're smart, you'll run. It was no big deal.

—**RED GRANGE**, FOOTBALL PLAYER

Most people would succeed in small things if they were not troubled with great ambitions.

—**HENRY WADSWORTH LONGFELLOW**, POET

Great issues develop from small beginnings.

—**NORMAN VINCENT PEALE**, MINISTER AND WRITER

It is by attempting to reach the top at a single leap that so much misery is caused in the world.

—**WILLIAM COBBETT**, JOURNALIST

Much rain wears the marble.

—**WILLIAM SHAKESPEARE**, PLAYWRIGHT

If you get yourself too engrossed in things over which you have no control, it's going to adversely affect the things over which you have control.

—**JOHN WOODEN**, BASKETBALL COACH

I was 6'4, 155 pounds when I was in high school. Just please do the math. It doesn't work out. That doesn't add up to a human being. And I was very awkward. And I think that's where you develop your sense of humor. You have to develop a sense of humor when you look like that. It looked like the circus was in town and staying.

—**CONAN O'BRIEN**, WRITER AND TALK SHOW HOST

Laughter can be many things—sometimes a medicine, sometimes a weapon, depending on who's administering it.

—**ROBIN WILLIAMS**, AWARD-WINNING ACTOR AND COMEDIAN

227

THE 28TH NINJA SECRET TO BEING A TOTALLY UNSTOPPABLE KID

HOW TO WALK A TIGHTROPE
(TAKING LIFE ONE STEP AT A TIME)

You've probably heard it said a gazillion times: Time flies. But the truth is, time doesn't just fly—it launches into hyperdrive and never stops.

Somehow we convince ourselves that if we can just blow through this month or this year, well, then everything will be different. Everything will be *better*. When you transfer schools, life will be better. When you have a steady girlfriend, life will be better. If you make the cut on a team at school, life will be better.

You can spend days and weeks and months obsessing about the future. Meanwhile, all those days and weeks and months are gone! And what have you done except dwell on something that's not even *here*? Burning time is worse than burning money because you can always earn more cash. Time can't be bought, borrowed, or sold.

It's important to focus on—and enjoy—what's right in front of you. Your favorite sports season, a weekend of chillaxin with your besties, or the great meal your parents just put on the table. The life you've been given isn't playing on DVD—there's no rewind button. Once these moments are gone, they're nothing but memories.

All this stop-and-smell-the-roses talk is hard to truly appreciate until you're sitting in a rocking chair adjusting your hearing aid. Some people need a few wrinkles to be convinced that they should stop wishing away time.

You, on the other hand, have the benefit of either wishing your days away, or taking things one step at a time. ●

This world, it's rough-and-tumble. It's wild and ragged. And the point is, are you confronting life? Are you in present time?

—**TOM CRUISE**, STAR OF THE *MISSION IMPOSSIBLE* MOVIES

When I was a kid in Toronto, I had no idea I'd be employed and remain employed. It's more like driving at night with beams that are low on the ground. You really can't see too far ahead.

—**MIKE MYERS**, WRITER, ACTOR, AND STAR OF *AUSTIN POWERS*

Only put off until tomorrow what you are willing to die having left undone.

—**PABLO PICASSO**, SURREALIST ARTIST

People always ask me, "What's the plan?" There is no plan. I go to what fascinates me next.

—**RIDLEY SCOTT**, DIRECTOR

I'm still at the beginning of my career. It's all a little new, and I'm still learning as I go.

—**ORLANDO BLOOM**, ACTOR STARRING IN
    LORD OF THE RINGS

This—the immediate, everyday, and present experience—is *it*, the entire and ultimate point for the existence of a universe.

—**ALAN WATTS**, PHILOSOPHER

I try to learn from the past, but I plan for the future by focusing exclusively on the present. That's where the fun is.

—**DONALD TRUMP**, ENTREPRENUER

If you spend your whole life waiting for the storm, you'll never enjoy the sunshine.

—**MORRIS WEST**, WRITER

Every moment that I am centered in the future, I suffer a temporary loss of this life.

—**HUGH PRATHER**, MINISTER

Each day is a new day, try to make it mean something. Set your long-term goals and achieve them by a day-in, day-out effort. That's the way you build a life.

—JOHN GLENN, ASTRONAUT AND SENATOR

I have the happiness of the passing moment, and what more can mortal ask?

—GEORGE R. GISSING, WRITER

He who does not get fun and enjoyment out of every day . . . needs to reorganize his life.

—GEORGE MATTHEW ADAMS, COLUMNIST

This is a tough game. There are times when you've got to play hurt, when you've got to block out the pain.

—SHAQUILLE O'NEAL, BASKETBALL PLAYER

To live only for some future goal is shallow. It's the sides of the mountain that sustain life, not the top.

—ROBERT M. PIRSIG, WRITER AND PHILOSOPHER

It is now, and in this world, that we must live.

—ANDRE GIDE, WRITER

People who postpone happiness are like children
who try chasing rainbows in an effort to find the pot
of gold at the rainbow's end. . . . Your life will never
be fulfilled until you are happy here and now.

—KEN KEYES, JR., MOTIVATIONAL SPEAKER

Listen once in a while. It's amazing what you can hear.

—RUSSELL BAKER, WRITER AND HUMORIST

An ounce of action is worth a ton of theory.

—FRIEDRICH ENGELS, PHILOSOPHER

Life is not lost by dying; life is lost minute by minute,
day by day, in all the thousand small, uncaring ways.

—STEPHEN VINCENT BENET, WRITER

I believe that only one person in a thousand knows
the trick of really living in the present.

—STORM JAMESON, WRITER

The cares of today are seldom those of tomorrow.

—**WILLIAM COWPER**, POET

Life's a journey, not a destination.

—**STEVEN TYLER**, MUSICIAN AND FRONTMAN
FOR AEROSMITH

One of the most glorious messes in the world is the
mess created in the living room on Christmas Day.
Don't clean it up too quickly.

—**ANDY ROONEY**, HUMORIST

Apologizes are pointless, regrets come too late. What
matters is you can move on, you can grow.

—**KELSEY GRAMMER**, ACTOR STARRING IN
FRASIER

YOU MUST OVERCOME YOUR FEAR.

GOOD! NOW...*TAKE OFF THE BLINDFOLD.*

HEY! I WAS ONLY *INCHES* FROM THE *GROUND!*

EXACTLY. FEAR DOESN'T COME FROM HEIGHTS...

...IT COMES FROM YOUR MIND!

THE 29TH NINJA SECRET TO
BEING A TOTALLY UNSTOPPABLE KID

HOW TO FIND YOUR
SECRET STRENGTH

(OVERCOMING FEARS)

If you're looking for an example of courage, don't head to the DVD counter. Batman, Superman, and Spiderman? They're a bunch of wimps compared to a kid who stands up to the school bully or confronts his best friend about shoplifting.

Some people have a funny—and unfortunate—way of defining bravery. There's so much focus on physical acts. Of course, there's no denying that you need guts to climb mountains or race cars, but courage is more than muscle and speed. Bravery comes from your heart and mind, too.

Consider these important aspects of superhero status:

Preparation means you'll need smaller doses of bravery. It takes courage to perform a saxophone solo during the band concert in front of a packed house. But think of it this way: It takes *more* courage if you're winging that solo and *less* courage if you've practiced.

Stay positive. If you believe in yourself, and if you believe in what you're doing, you'll be able to tackle just about any challenge—whether it's physical or mental. If you let doubt crack your spirit, you'll struggle to accomplish anything.

Praise others for their courage. You know how hard it is to stand up in front of the class and give a speech. If your buddy nails his speech without breaking a sweat, let him know. It's important to be recognized.

So forget about the mask and cape. You have the recipe for courage inside your heart and mind. Famous men agree—check out what they have to say about being brave.●

When things get bad—and that's just life, there's always going to be those dark moments—the only real light is the inner light. You have to have some kind of belief that there is a divine spirit that is watching over you and is going to provide you with peace of mind.

—**SYLVESTER STALLONE,** ACTOR AND STAR OF *ROCKY*

Necessity makes even the timid brave.

—**SALLUST,** ROMAN HISTORIAN

Strong people are made by opposition, like kites that go up against the wind.

—**FRANK HARRIS,** WRITER

I've always had my freedom. The price I paid for it was popularity and money.

—**JIM BROWN,** FOOTBALL PLAYER

It is foolish and wrong to mourn the men who died. Rather we should thank God that such men lived.

—**GEORGE S. PATTON,** GENERAL

Safer is not a good thing.

—**ROBIN WILLIAMS**, AWARD-WINNING
ACTOR AND COMEDIAN

Courage is contagious. When a brave man takes a
stand, the spines of others are often stiffened.

—**BILLY GRAHAM**, MINISTER

Go to the edge of the cliff and jump off. Build your
wings on the way down.

—**RAY BRADBURY**, AUTHOR OF
FAHRENHEIT 451

My folks both survived Auschwitz. They met after the
war, they came to New York without a nickel in their
pocket, yet they both had a pretty strong passion for
living and wanted to give the best that they could
to their kids. That's where I get a lot of my strength
from.

—**LOUIS SCHWARTZBERG**, DOCUMENTARY
FILMMAKER

Every failure made me more confident. Because I wanted even more to achieve things, as revenge. To show that I could.

—**ROMAN POLANSKI**, DIRECTOR OF SUCH
FILMS AS *ROSEMARY'S BABY*

Difficulties should act as a tonic. They should spur us to greater exertion.

—**B. C. FORBES**, PUBLISHER

You don't accomplish much by swimming with the mainstream. Hell, a dead fish can do that.

—**KINKY FRIEDMAN**, SONGWRITER

Be brave enough to live creatively. The creative is the place where no one else has ever been. You have to leave the city of your comfort and go into the wilderness of your intuition. What you will discover will be wonderful. What you will discover will be yourself.

—**ALAN ALDA**, ACTOR STARRING IN *MASH*

Difficulties are meant to rouse, not discourage. The human spirit is to grow strong by conflict.

—**WILLIAM ELLERY CHANNING**,
THEOLOGIAN

Adversity causes some men to break, others to break records.

—**WILLIAM A. WARD**, WRITER

Never to suffer would have been never to have been blessed.

—**EDGAR ALLAN POE**, WRITER

If we survive danger, it steels our courage more than anything else.

—**REINHOLD NIEBUHR**, THEOLOGIAN

Adversity is another way to measure the greatness of individuals. I never had a crisis that didn't make me stronger.

—**LOU HOLTZ**, FORMER NCAA FOOTBALL
PLAYER AND NFL HEAD COACH

You're never done. You're never done. And the moment you think you're done, you're an idiot. Straight up. If you think you're ever done, you're a fool.

—CHRIS COLE, PROFESSIONAL SKATER

To accept whatever comes, regardless of the consequences, is to be unafraid.

—JOHN CAGE, COMPOSER AND MUSICAL PIONEER

I tried to stay positive and never felt sorry for myself.

—REM MURRAY, HOCKEY PLAYER

The greatest test of courage on earth is to bear defeat without losing heart.

—ROBERT G. INGERSOLL, POLITICIAN

Courage is a perfect sensibility of the measure of danger, and a mental willingness to endure it.

—WILLIAM T. SHERMAN, GENERAL

WHAT TO DO WHEN THINGS DISAPPEAR

(COPING WITH LOSS AND CHANGE)

Your social studies teacher calls on you during class and asks a question about current affairs. You know the answer, so no big deal. You open your mouth and, in front of the entire class, your voice explodes into a hideous SQUEAK. Everyone laughs—everyone but you.

The roller coaster voice experience is your body changing and growing. And it's all the proof you need to know that change is not always pleasant. Whether you like it or not, everything is constantly changing—your body, your mind, your world. Your best buddies today are not the same kids you played with in kindergarten. Your favorite movies, food, and video games are constantly changing. And maybe you're living in a different house than when you were a baby. Maybe your family even moved from one state to another—and then moved back again!

Some of the changes you face—like the death of a family member or your parents' divorce—are going to be among the most difficult experiences of your life. You need to take care of yourself during those tough times and lean on your friends for support. You need to give yourself time to grieve for the loss of what was familiar and comfortable. Slowly, you'll transition into a new way of living. If you find that you're not making that transition, you need to turn to adults you trust and get their help.

Usually, change isn't so dramatic and painful. Change makes life interesting, and sometimes it's actually fun. Since you can't stop change, you might as well try to embrace it. ●

With my sunglasses on, I'm Jack Nicholson. Without them, I'm fat and 60.

—JACK NICHOLSON, ACTOR AND STAR OF
THE SHINING

People don't resist change. They resist being changed!

—PETER SENGE, SCIENTIST

It is a known science fact that, no matter how good your yearbook photo looks now, after 15 years of being pressed up against somebody else's face in the dark and mysterious yearbook environment, it will transmutate itself into a humiliating picture of a total goober.

—DAVE BARRY, HUMORIST

You must be the change you wish to see in the world.

—MAHATMA GANDHI, PEACE ACTIVIST

I fear there will be no future for those who do not change.

—LOUIS L'AMOUR, WRITER

Tomorrow is the mysterious, unknown guest.

    —HENRY WADSWORTH LONGFELLOW, POET

Boredom is the most horrible of wolves.

    —JEAN GIONO, WRITER

They always say that time changes things, but you actually have to change them yourself.

    —ANDY WARHOL, ARTIST

I love being a part of *High School Musical*, I wish I could do it forever but everyone's got to grow up.

    —ZAC EFRON, ACTOR

There are no conditions to which a man cannot become accustomed.

    —LEO TOLSTOY, WRITER BEST KNOWN FOR
      NOVELS *ANNA KARENINA* AND *WAR AND*
      PEACE

We cannot change anything unless we accept it.

    —CARL JUNG, PSYCHIATRIST

Man adapts himself to everything, to the best and the worst.

—JOSE ORTEGA Y GASSET, PHILOSOPHER

We don't do a lot of violent shows. When I started in television, breaking a pencil was a violent act.

—AARON SPELLING, TELEVISION PRODUCER

The art of living does not consist in preserving and clinging to a particular mood of happiness, but in allowing happiness to change its form . . . happiness, like a child, must be allowed to grow up.

—CHARLES L. MORGAN, WRITER

Readjusting is a painful process, but most of us need it one time or another.

—ARTHUR CHRISTOPHER BENSON, WRITER

I liked being a teenager, but I would not go back for all the tea in China.

—ROB LOWE, ACTOR STARRING IN
ST. ELMO'S FIRE

Life is 10 percent what you make it, and 90 percent how you take it.

—IRVING BERLIN, COMPOSER

You're just an actor. You're gonna be replaced in about five, six years. People start thinking "Oh, Hollywood can't work without me—I'm a star!" They'll do just fine without you. Your tickets are for Podunk tomorrow on the 9:30 a.m.

—JOHNNY KNOXVILLE, ACTOR STARRING IN THE MTV SERIES *JACKASS*

I've gotta keep writing. But where's the next step, where do you go? But at my age, you start to get tired. You're not full of piss and vinegar. The vinegar's all gone

—MICKEY SPILLANE, WRITER

You can do these things until they carry you out on a stretcher or you can get out while you're still doing good.

—JAY LENO, COMEDIAN AND FORMER HOST OF THE *TONIGHT SHOW*

Any change, even a change for the better, is always accompanied by drawbacks and discomforts.

—ARNOLD BENNETT, WRITER

Change is what people fear most.

—FYODOR DOSTOYEVSKY, WRITER BEST
KNOWN FOR *CRIME AND PUNISHMENT* AND
THE BROTHERS KARAMAZOV

My comedy is different every time I do it. I don't know what the hell I'm doing

—ADAM SANDLER, COMEDIAN, *SATURDAY
NIGHT LIVE* CAST MEMBER, AND FILM
ACTOR

Once you are labeled the best, you want to stay up there, and you can't do it by loafing around. If I don't keep changing, I'm history.

—LARRY BIRD, BASKETBALL PLAYER AND
THREE-TIME NBA MVP

WHAT TO DO WHEN THE DARK SIDE WINS

(COPING WITH SETBACKS)

Sometimes life beats you up. Your parents won't let you go to the best party of the year, the one where all the cool people from school will be Friday night. *Bam—a jab to the chest.* You're getting a D in science class. *Wham—an upper cut to the jaw.* Your grandfather is diagnosed with cancer. *Smash—a hook to the ribs.* You are definitely down for the count.

But you can't stay down. When things aren't going your way, it's easy to feel blue. It's easy to get pumped full of anger and frustration. What's hard is working through tough times while keeping your cool. Here are some tough-times survival tips:

Let yourself feel blue—or angry—for a while. It's unhealthy to deny those feelings and pretend they don't exist. The point is to not let the negativity linger too long.

Keep your perspective. Nobody wants to bring home a report card with a big red D, but it's something you can improve. Make a plan to change your grade to a C—or even a B—by getting some help from your teacher before school and making more time to study.

Focus on the positive things in your life. For every bad thing that happens, you can probably find six good things if you just look for them.

Ask for help if you need it. Your friends are probably great listeners, but if you're really struggling, you might need the help of a teacher, school counselor, or parent.

Tough times are inevitable, but you'll get through them because you're smart and resourceful. ●

Things change rapidly, and life gets better in an instant.

> —JON STEWART, COMEDIAN AND TALK SHOW HOST

In Hollywood, you just kind of fail upwards.

> —KEVIN SMITH, DIRECTOR

I'm retiring because there are more pleasant things to do than beat up people.

> —MUHAMMAD ALI, CHAMPION BOXER

Humor is the instinct for taking pain playfully.

> —MAX EASTMAN, WRITER

There are more serious problems in life than financial ones, and I've had a lot of those. I've been broke before, and will be again. Heartbroke? That's serious. Lose a few bucks? That's not.

> —WILLIE NELSON, COUNTRY MUSIC SINGER

The cure for grief is motion.

>—**ELBERT HUBBARD**, WRITER AND
>PHILOSOPHER

If you want to see the sun shine, you have to weather the storm.

>—**FRANK LANE**, BASEBALL MANAGER

Anything other than death is a minor injury.

>—**BILL MUNCEY**, HYDROPLANE RACER

Forget the times of your distress, but never forget what they taught you.

>—**HERBERT GASSER**, PHYSIOLOGIST

Bad times have a scientific value. These are occasions a good learner would not miss.

>—**RALPH WALDO EMERSON**, PHILOSOPHER
>AND POET

I don't understand the ones that have no sense of hope and invest in hate. That's not gonna work out, you know? It's a waste of your time!

> —**TOM PETTY**, MUSICIAN AND FRONTMAN IN
> TOM PETTY AND THE HEARTBREAKERS

Somehow, you need to cling to your optimism. Always look for the silver lining. Always look for the best in people.

> —**RICHIE SAMBORA**, MUSICIAN AND LEAD
> GUITARIST OF BON JOVI

You have to have hope. It's the only way to go on.

> —**PIERCE BROSNAN**, ACTOR WHO STARRED
> AS JAMES BOND

Humor is just another defense against the universe.

> —**MEL BROOKS**, WRITER, DIRECTOR,
> AND ACTOR

I'll go anywhere as long as it's forward.

> —**DAVID LIVINGSTONE**, EXPLORER

Divorce is painful because it is unknown to a child. You don't have a context for it, so it destroys the very notion of context, because the only context you know as a child is family.

—**BOB WOODWARD**, JOURNALIST

The most unhappy of all men is he who believes himself to be so.

—**DAVID HUME**, PHILOSOPHER

The mind in its own place, and in itself can make a heaven of hell, a hell of heaven.

—**JOHN MILTON**, POET

Desperation is a necessary ingredient to learning anything, or creating anything. Period. If you ain't desperate at some point, you ain't interesting.

—**JIM CARREY**, AWARD-WINNING FILM ACTOR AND COMEDIAN

When the gods go after you, they really know where to strike

—**LEON FLEISHER**, MUSICIAN

The ideal man bears the accidents of life with dignity and grace, making the best of circumstances.

—**ARISTOTLE**, GREEK PHILOSOPHER

I would have never amounted to anything were it not for adversity. I was forced to come up the hard way.

—**J.C. PENNEY**, BUSINESSMAN

Acceptance of what has happened is the first step to overcoming the consequence of any misfortune.

—**WILLIAM JAMES**, PSYCHOLOGIST

The stupid neither forgive nor forget; the naïve forgive and forget; the wise forgive, but do not forget.

—**THOMAS SZASZ**, PSYCHIATRIST

CONTINUED ON PG 268

THE 32ND NINJA SECRET TO
BEING A TOTALLY UNSTOPPABLE KID

HOW TO ENJOY
A GOOD MYSTERY

(ACCEPTING THE UNKNOWN)

You have a date with destiny. Avoid arguments with your closest friends. Your bold spirit attracts change. Fortune cookies—filled with lame sayings that could apply to anyone—are still something that people love to crack open. Know why? Because we all dig mysteries.

Think about it. Every night when your head hits the pillow, you ask yourself one big question: What's going to happen tomorrow? Maybe it will be another text message from that one cute girl at school. Or an invitation to a party Friday night. Or news that your family is going somewhere fun over winter break.

That one big question then leads to lots of little ones: *Why* is that cute girl texting you? Does she want to hang out? Could she possibly like you? You know, *really* like you?

Thinking about those kinds of things can be a blast. But worrying about more serious things—like a family problem, or why one of your friends is dissing you—is nothing any of us enjoy. If trying to decode life's mysteries has you so wired that you can't even sleep, it's best to just relax and enjoy the ride. None of us can predict or control the future, no matter how many fortune cookies we open. ●

You can't connect the dots looking forward; you can only connect them looking backwards. So you have to trust that the dots will somehow connect in your future.

—**STEVE JOBS**, COFOUNDER AND CEO OF APPLE

In animation you can create so many little mysteries.

—**TREY PARKER**, CO-CREATOR OF *SOUTH PARK*

Mountaineering is a relentless pursuit. One climbs further and further yet never reaches the destination. Perhaps that is what gives it its own particular charm. One is constantly searching for something never to be found.

—**HERMANN BUHL**, MOUNTAIN CLIMBER

The unknown is what it is. Accept that it's unknown, and it's plain sailing.

—**JOHN LENNON**, LEGENDARY MEMBER OF THE BEATLES AND FIRST PERSON TO APPEAR ON THE COVER OF *ROLLING STONE*

Mystery creates wonder and wonder is the basis of man's desire to understand.

> —**NEIL ARMSTRONG**, ASTRONAUT AND FIRST MAN TO SET FOOT ON THE MOON

The most beautiful thing we can experience is the mysterious.

> —**ALBERT EINSTEIN**, PHYSICIST BEST KNOWN FOR HIS THEORY OF RELATIVITY

I think you end up doing the stuff you were supposed to do at the time you were supposed to do it.

> —**ROBERT DOWNEY, JR.**, ACTOR, STAR OF THE *IRON MAN* MOVIES

The game is most fun when you are experimenting.

> —**JACK NICKLAUS**, PROFESSIONAL GOLFER

In the book of life's questions, the answers are not in the back.

> —**CHARLES SCHULZ**, CREATOR OF CHARLIE BROWN AND *PEANUTS*

It's a surprise.

—**MASASHI KISHIMOTO**, MANGA ARTIST,
CREATOR OF *NARUTO*

I don't know what I'm doing tomorrow. I completely
live in the now, not in the past, not in the future.

—**HEATH LEDGER**, ACTOR WHO PLAYED THE
JOKER IN *THE DARK KNIGHT*

When I feel that a painting has its own voice and is
coming alive, I want to live with it, talk to it, quarrel
with it, and agree with it. In other words, I don't want
to put my signature to it, and bring the experience to
an end.

—**ALBERTO SUGHI**, PAINTER

The less you know, the more you believe.

—**BONO**, LEAD SINGER OF U2

Time is a circus always packing up and moving away.

—**BEN HECHT**, SCREENWRITER AND
DIRECTOR

Today is the first day of the rest of your life.
—**ABBIE HOFFMAN**, ACTIVIST

Some people think that there's a music rulebook that was written a long time ago. BR549 never owned a copy of that handbook, and never will.
—**SHAW WILSON**, BR549 BAND MEMBER

Realize life as an end in itself. Functioning is all there is.
—**OLIVER WENDELL HOLMES, JR.**, SUPREME COURT JUDGE

The true beauty of this planet is its diversity, not its sameness.
—**ROBERT BALLARD**, EXPLORER

I feel beautiful music should be shared, not hoarded; it teaches us to feel what we might not have felt. It touches our souls and helps us understand the world in a more imaginative and precise way.
—**LANG LANG**, PIANIST

I love to travel. Much more than I've ever enjoyed getting anywhere. Arrival is overrated. Moving is much more exciting.

> —**JERRY SEINFELD**, COMEDIAN, ACTOR, AND STAR OF *SEINFELD*

We should consider every day lost on which we have not danced at least once.

> —**FRIEDRICH NIETZSCHE**, PHILOSOPHER

I dream of bonefish, I dream of salmon, I dream of casting for them, I dream of the beautiful spots I've seen.

> —**TED WILLIAMS**, BASEBALL PLAYER

THE END

Sketches

The very first sketches of Atticus made him look older, while his mum looked young and cute instead.

mum

ATTICUS

Atticus was described as an "emo" kid, so perhaps that's why he looked the way he did.

Ninja, on the other hand, was meant to look just a tad exotic.

NINJA

COACH

Coach's design was based on "Chief Porter", a character from "In Odd We Trust".

Sketches (Con't)

ATTICUS (2)

mum (2)

In the revised sketches, Atticus ended up looking a lot younger. He kept the "emo" hairstyle, but he's definitely cuter-looking!

Mum looks less cute but more "mom-looking", while Ninja gains a fuller head of hair. I like these designs a lot more the second time around - they fit the characters a lot more.

NINJA (2)

ABOUT THE CREATORS

Steve Deger has served as a volunteer speaker, fundraiser, and "Big" for Big Brothers Big Sisters of America. He is the co-creator of the *Positive Quotation* series, which has sold more than half a million copies and spent more than two years on the national bestseller charts for reference, self-help, and juvenile nonfiction books. He lives in Minneapolis, Minnesota.

Queenie Chan was born in Hong Kong and emigrated to Australia when she was six years old. She is author of the three-volume manga *The Dreaming*, which has been translated into four languages. She is the illustrator and co-creator (with Dean Koontz) of the Odd Thomas graphic novels.